HEALTH CARE ISSUES, COSTS AND ACCESS

PRESCRIPTION DRUG PRICING

COST AND CONTROL CONCERNS

Health Care Issues, Costs and Access

Additional books in this series can be found on Nova's website under the Series tab.

Additional E-books in this series can be found on Nova's website under the E-books tab.

Drug Transit and Distribution, Interception and Control

Additional books in this series can be found on Nova's website under the Series tab.

Additional E-books in this series can be found on Nova's website under the E-books tab.

HEALTH CARE ISSUES, COSTS AND ACCESS

PRESCRIPTION DRUG PRICING

COST AND CONTROL CONCERNS

JONATHAN R.DICKSON
AND
AMY M. WOEBLER
EDITORS

Nova Science Publishers, Inc.
New York

Library of Congress Cataloging-in-Publication Data

Prescription drug pricing : cost and control concerns / editors, Jonathan R. Dickson and Amy M. Woebler.
p. ; cm.
Includes bibliographical references and index.
ISBN 978-1-61324-639-9 (hardcover : alk. paper) 1. Prescription pricing--United States. 2. Medical economics--United States. I. Dickson, Jonathan R. II. Woebler, Amy M.
[DNLM: 1. Drug Costs--United States. 2. Prescription Drugs--economics--United States. 3. Costs and Cost Analysis--United States. 4. Drug Industry--economics--United States. QV 736]
RS100.P73 2011
615'.1--dc23

2011015645

Published by Nova Science Publishers, Inc. † New York

CONTENTS

PREFACE

The growing cost of brand-name prescription drugs can be a burden on patients, payers and providers of health care, particularly when price increases are large and occur suddenly. Controlling rising prescription drug prices helps to ensure that patients can afford medically necessary and sometimes life-saving medication, and to moderate costs for hospitals and third-party payers such as insurance plans and state and federal governments. This book examines prescription drug pricing costs and control concerns with a focus on extraordinary price increases for brand-name prescription drugs, as well as the characteristics and factors that contributed to this price increase.

Chapter 1- Prescription drug spending in 2009 totaled approximately $250 billion, of which $78 billion—or about 31 percent—was spent by the federal government. Prescription drug spending by the federal government, patients, and third-party payers, including employers, is driven by many factors, including the prices paid for drugs. In 2007 we reported on trends in retail prices—known as usual and customary (U&C) prices—for prescription drugs. We found that the average U&C price for the commonly used brand-name prescription drugs we reviewed increased about 6 percent per year from January 2000 through January 2007. Some media reports have suggested that prescription drug prices may have increased more during the debate leading up to passage of the Patient Protection and Affordable Care Act (PPACA) in March 2010 compared to other recent years.

Chapter 2- The growing cost of brand-name prescription drugs—FDA-approved drug products that typically have patent protection—is a concern for patients, payers, and providers of health care—particularly when price increases are large and occur suddenly. A 2008 congressional hearing by the

Joint Economic Committee drew attention to some small market prescription drugs that had an extraordinary price increase—a price increase of 100 percent or more at a single point in time.

Chapter 3- Millions of individuals receive prescription drugs through federal programs. The increasing cost of prescription drugs has put pressure to control drug spending on federal programs such as the Federal Employees Health Benefits Program (FEHBP), Medicare Part D, the Department of Veterans Affairs (VA), the Department of Defense (DOD), and Medicaid. Prescription drug spending within the FEHBP in particular, which provides health and drug coverage to about 8 million federal employees, retirees, and their dependents, has been a significant contributor to FEHBP cost and premium growth. The Office of Personnel Management (OPM), which administers the FEHBP, predicted that prescription drugs would continue to be a primary driver of program costs in 2009.

Chapter 4 – This is a statement of U.S. Senator Amy Klobuchar.

Chapter 5 – This is a statement of Senator Charles E. Schumer, Chairman, Joint Economic Committee.

Chapter 6 – This is a statement of Madeline M. Carpinelli, research fellow and Stephen W. Schondelmeyer Professor and Director, before Joint Economic Committee, United States Congress.

Chapter 7 – This is a statement of Alan L. Goldbloom, MD, President and CEO, Children's Hospitals and Clinics of Minnesota before Joint Economic Committee.

Chapter 8 – This is a statement of Danielle Foltz, mother of Trevor Foltz.

Chapter 9- It is well recognized that an incumbent may deter potential competitors by taking strategic action that reduces the profitability of entry. However, the use of price as a strategic entry deterrent is controversial since it may be profitable for the incumbent to raise price after entry has occurred, making its commitment to a low, entry-deterring price incredible. Depending on the theoretical model used to explain the link between the incumbent's pre-entry price and an entrant's expected profits, the effect of potential competition can vary from being extremely strong to entirely ineffectual in constraining market power. This wide range of theoretical outcomes highlights the need for empirical analysis to determine the real-world importance of potential competition.

In: Prescription Drug Pricing
Editors: J. R. Dickson, A. M. Woebler
ISBN: 978-1-61324-639-9

Chapter 1

PRESCRIPTION DRUGS: TRENDS IN USUAL AND CUSTOMARY PRICES FOR COMMONLY USED DRUGS

United States Government Accountability Office

February 10, 2011

Congressional Requesters

Subject: *Prescription Drugs: Trends in Usual and Customary Prices for Commonly Used Drugs*

Prescription drug spending in 2009 totaled approximately $250 billion, of which $78 billion—or about 31 percent—was spent by the federal government.[1] Prescription drug spending by the federal government, patients, and third-party payers, including employers, is driven by many factors, including the prices paid for drugs. In 2007 we reported on trends in retail prices—known as usual and customary (U&C) prices—for prescription drugs.[2] We found that the average U&C price for the commonly used brand-name prescription drugs we reviewed increased about 6 percent per year from January 2000 through January 2007.[3] Some media reports[4] have suggested that prescription drug prices may have increased more during the debate leading up to passage of the Patient Protection and Affordable Care Act (PPACA) in March 2010 compared to other recent years.[5]

We were requested to examine recent trends in drug prices for brand-name and generic pharmaceuticals. In this report, we (1) examine U&C price trends for commonly used prescription drugs from 2006 through the first quarter of 2010, the latest available data at the time of our analysis, and compare these trends to those of other medical consumer goods and services, and (2) examine price trends using drug prices other than U&C. You also asked us to provide information on the extent to which prices for individual brand-name drugs changed over the course of this analysis period. We have provided this information in an enclosure.

In order to determine U&C price trends from 2006 through the first quarter of 2010, we selected four baskets of drugs that were commonly used by consumers during our analysis period. To select our baskets, we used prescription drug utilization data from the Blue Cross Blue Shield Federal Employee Program (BCBS FEP), a large, nationwide insurance plan that covers nearly 5 million individuals.[6] We selected the first basket of drugs based on drug name in order to examine overall price trends of both brand-name and generic drugs. We used BCBS FEP utilization data to identify 100 commonly used drugs, and we considered the brand-name and generic versions to be distinct drugs with distinct levels of utilization.[7] We selected the second and third baskets of drugs to examine trends for brand-name and for generic drugs separately. The second and third baskets of drugs were subsets of the first basket and contained the 55 brand-name and the 45 generic drugs,[8] respectively, from the first basket of 100 drugs. We selected the fourth basket of drugs in order to account for the growing national shift in consumer utilization from brand-name to generic versions of drugs. We used BCBS FEP utilization data to again select 100 commonly used drugs—this time based on the active ingredient rather than drug name.[9] In selecting this fourth basket of drugs based on active ingredient, we considered the brand-name and generic versions of drugs with the same active ingredient to be the same drug. The degree of overlap between the contents of the fourth basket and the first basket was high: at least 95 percent of the utilization in one basket was also in the other.

To report the U&C price trends, we calculated quarterly changes in the average price of each basket of drugs from 2006 through the first quarter of 2010 using quarterly price indexes. For each index, we used the first quarter of 2006 as a baseline with an assigned value of 100 and calculated change over each quarter as an expressed value above or below 100. We relied on U&C data from Pennsylvania's Pharmaceutical Assistance Contract for the Elderly (PACE) program as our main data source because they were actual retail prices that pharmacies charged to cash-paying consumers for prescription drugs and were available across our entire analysis period.

We compared the drug price indexes we constructed to the average annual change from 2006 through first quarter 2010 in the consumer price index for medical goods and services (medical CPI) and in the broader consumer price index for all consumer goods for urban consumers (CPI-U), both of which are publicly available from the Bureau of Labor Statistics. The medical CPI—which includes prescription and nonprescription drugs, medical equipment, and services—makes up about 6.5 percent of the CPI-U; the remaining 93.5 percent of this broader index reflects changes in prices for other (nonmedical) consumer goods and services.[10]

In order to determine price trends using drug prices other than U&C, we created three separate price indexes using three additional measures of drug prices. We calculated the indexes using these three additional measures of drug prices for our first basket of 100 drugs following the same methodology used to construct the U&C price index. We used average wholesale prices (AWP), which are "list prices" reported by manufacturers; average manufacturer prices (AMP), which are average prices paid to manufacturers by wholesalers and other purchasers; and Medicare Part D Plan Finder negotiated prices (Part D), which are prices negotiated between participating Part D plans and pharmacies for Medicare Part D consumers.[11] We obtained AWP data from Red Book[12] and both AMP and Part D Plan Finder data from the Centers for Medicare & Medicaid Services (CMS).

The results of our analyses are limited to the commonly used prescription drugs in our baskets and cannot be generalized to all prices nationally for all drugs. In addition, the U&C analyses are limited to prices reported by retail pharmacies in Pennsylvania to the PACE program and cannot be generalized to all U&C prices nationally for all drugs. We reviewed data from BCBS FEP, CMS, Red Book, and the PACE program for reasonableness and consistency, including screening for outlier prices and examining possible reasons for inconsistencies between the data sources. We also reviewed documentation and talked to data providers about steps they take to ensure data reliability. We determined that these data were sufficiently reliable for our purposes. We conducted this performance audit from April 2010 through January 2011 in accordance with generally accepted government auditing standards. Those standards require that we plan and perform the audit to obtain sufficient, appropriate evidence to provide a reasonable basis for our findings and conclusions based on our audit objectives. We believe that the evidence obtained provides a reasonable basis for our findings and conclusions based on our audit objectives. (See enc. I for a detailed discussion of our scope and methodology and enc. II for a listing of the drugs in each basket.)

RESULTS IN BRIEF

We found that the U&C price index for our first basket of 100 commonly used prescription drugs increased at an average annual rate of 6.6 percent from 2006 through the first quarter of 2010 compared with a 3.8 percent average annual increase in the medical CPI.[13] The increase in the price index from the first quarter of 2009 through the first quarter of 2010—prior to passage of health reform in March 2010—was 5.9 percent, less than the increase for the 2 years prior but higher than in 2006. We also found that the U&C price index for our second basket of 55 brand-name drugs increased at an average annual rate of 8.3 percent during our time period. In contrast, the U&C price index for our third basket of 45 generic drugs decreased at an average annual rate of 2.6 percent. Finally, when shifts in consumer utilization between brand-name and generic versions of the same drug were included in the analysis using our fourth basket of drugs selected by active ingredient, the U&C price index increased about 2.6 percent per year, a much lower rate than the 6.6 percent annual increase observed when shifts in utilization were not included.

We found that price trends for the 100 drugs in our first basket as measured using drug prices other than U&C also increased from 2006 through the first quarter of 2010, but at a somewhat slower rate than the 6.6 percent rate for the U&C price index. For example, the AWP price index increased at an average annual rate of 6.0 percent while the AMP price index increased at an average annual rate of 5.3 percent. The Part D price index—which was measured from 2007 through the first quarter of 2010—increased at an average annual rate of 6.8 percent, slightly less than the U&C price index of 7.0 percent when measured across the same period.

For additional details on our results, see enclosure III. We also provide information on the extent to which prices for individual brand-name drugs changed over the course of our analysis period in enclosure IV.

We did not obtain external comments on a draft of this report because we did not evaluate the programs of the organizations that provided us data.

As agreed with your offices, unless you publicly announce the contents of this report earlier, we plan no further distribution until 30 days from the report date. At that time, we will send copies of this report to relevant congressional committees and other interested members. The report also will be available at no charge on the GAO Web site at http://www.gao.gov.

If you or your staff have any questions regarding this report, please contact me at (202) 512-7114 or dickenj@gao.gov. Contact points for our Offices of Congressional Relations and Public Affairs may be found on the last page of this report. GAO staff members who made key contributions to this report are listed in enclosure V.

John E. Dicken
Director, Health Care
Enclosures – 5

List of Requesters

The Honorable Henry A. Waxman
Ranking Member
Committee on Energy and Commerce
House of Representatives

The Honorable Sander M. Levin
Ranking Member
Committee on Ways and Means
House of Representatives

The Honorable Pete Stark
Ranking Member
Subcommittee on Health
Committee on Ways and Means
House of Representatives

The Honorable John Lewis
Ranking Member
Subcommittee on Oversight
Committee on Ways and Means
House of Representatives
The Honorable Charles B. Rangel
House of Representatives

Enclosure I

Scope and Methodology

In order to determine usual and customary (U&C) price trends from 2006 through the first quarter of 2010, we selected four baskets of drugs that were commonly used by consumers during our analysis period.[14] To select our baskets, we used prescription drug utilization data from the Blue Cross Blue Shield Federal Employee Program (BCBS FEP), a large, nationwide insurance plan that covers nearly 5 million individuals.[15] We used data from the first quarter of 2006 to identify the most commonly dispensed 30-day supply for each drug and then used this quantity to determine the corresponding number of 30-day equivalents represented by each claim. We also used data from the Food and Drug Administration (FDA) and Red Book[16] to determine the brand-name or generic status of each drug at the beginning and end of our analysis period.

We selected the first basket of drugs based on drug name in order to examine overall price trends of both brand-name and generic drugs over our time period. We used BCBS FEP utilization data to select 100 commonly used drugs. We aggregated all claims with the same drug name, strength, route of administration, and dosage form in order to determine which drugs had the highest utilization. For example, all claims for "Zocor/10mg/oral/tablet" were combined as one drug. Using this drug name approach, the brand-name and generic versions of a drug were aggregated separately. For example, "Zocor/10mg/oral/tablet" and "simvastatin/10mg/oral/tablet" would be considered different drugs for purposes of our first basket because they have different names, even though they are the brand-name and generic versions of drugs containing the same active ingredient. The first drug basket contained 45 percent of all BCBS FEP 30-day equivalent prescriptions from the first quarter of 2006.

We selected the second and third baskets of drugs to examine trends for brand-name and for generic drugs separately. The second basket contained the 55 brand-name drugs from among the 100 commonly used drugs in the first basket, including 35 drugs that were single-source throughout our analysis period and 20 drugs that transitioned from single-source to brand-name multisource during the analysis period.[17] Because these two groups of drugs experienced similar price changes, we included both in our second basket of 55 brand-name drugs. The third basket contained the remaining 45 drugs from among the 100 commonly used drugs in the first basket, including 40 generic drugs and 5 drugs that were brand-name multisource during the entire analysis period.[18] Because these two groups of drugs experienced similar price changes, we included both in our third basket of 45 generic drugs.

We selected the fourth basket of drugs in order to account for the growing national shift in consumer utilization from brand-name to generic versions of drugs. We used BCBS FEP utilization data to again select 100 commonly used drugs—this time based on the active ingredient rather than drug name. We aggregated all claims with the same active ingredient, strength, route of administration, and dosage form. For example, all claims with "simvastatin" as the active ingredient and "10mg/oral/tablet" as the strength, route of administration, and dosage form were aggregated as a single drug. Using this approach, the brand-name and generic versions of a drug were combined and counted as one drug. For example, "Zocor/10mg/oral/tablet" and "simvastatin/10mg/oral/tablet" would be considered the same drug for purposes of this fourth basket because they are the brand-name and generic versions of drugs with the same active ingredient, even though they have different names. Under this approach for example, if consumer utilization of a particular drug in the basket shifts over time from a higher priced brand-name drug to a lower priced generic version of that drug, the generic version becomes increasingly more heavily weighted and thus will have an increasingly greater influence on the price change for the basket. The fourth drug basket contained 49 percent of all BCBS FEP 30-day equivalent prescriptions from the first quarter of 2006. The degree of overlap between the contents of the fourth basket and the first basket was high: at least 95 percent of the utilization in one basket was also in the other.

To report the U&C price trends, we calculated quarterly changes in the average price of each basket of drugs from 2006 through the first quarter of 2010 using utilization-weighted price indexes as described below. We relied on U&C prices as our main data source because they were actual retail prices that pharmacies charged to cash-paying consumers for prescription drugs and were available across our entire analysis period. The U&C prices were obtained from Pennsylvania's Pharmaceutical Assistance Contract for the Elderly (PACE) program.[19]

We used quarterly price indexes to compare drug prices from our baseline quarter (the first quarter of 2006) to prices in subsequent quarters. Price indexes were constructed by dividing the average quarterly price for a basket of drugs by the average price of the basket in the first quarter of 2006 and multiplying by 100. As a result, if the average price for a basket of drugs in a given quarter was higher than the average price in the baseline quarter, the resulting price index for that quarter was above 100, while an average quarterly price that was lower than the baseline price resulted in a price index below 100. To calculate average quarterly prices for each drug in our baskets, we first determined the average quarterly price for each national drug code (NDC) and multiplied that price by its BCBS FEP utilization for that quarter, then summed the results for all NDCs corresponding to a given drug. To calculate an average quarterly price for each basket, we multiplied the resulting quarterly price for each drug by its BCBS FEP utilization during the first quarter of 2006 and summed across all drugs in the basket. We then divided the resulting average quarterly price for each basket by its average price in the baseline quarter to produce quarterly price indexes with a baseline of 100 in the first quarter of 2006.

We compared the U&C price indexes we constructed to the average annual change from 2006 through first quarter 2010 in the consumer price index for medical goods and services (medical CPI) and in the broader consumer price index for all consumer goods for urban consumers (CPI-U), both of which are publicly available from the Bureau of Labor Statistics. The medical CPI—which includes prescription and nonprescription drugs, medical equipment, and services—makes up about 6.5 percent of the CPI-U; the remaining 93.5 percent of this broader index reflects changes in prices for other (nonmedical) consumer goods and services.[20]

In order to determine price trends using drug prices other than U&C, we created three separate price indexes using three additional measures of drug prices. We calculated the indexes for our first basket of 100 drugs following the same methodology used to construct the U&C price index. We used average wholesale price (AWP)—"list prices" reported by manufacturers—from Red Book; average manufacturer price (AMP)—average prices paid to manufacturers by wholesalers and other purchasers—from the Centers for Medicare & Medicaid Services (CMS); and Medicare Part D Plan Finder (Part D) data—prices negotiated between participating Part D plans and pharmacies for Medicare Part D consumers—from CMS.[21] The price index that we calculated using AMP data should be interpreted with caution for several reasons. First, CMS changed the calculation of AMP in accordance with the Deficit Reduction Act of 2005 starting on October 1, 2007.[22] In addition, we previously reported significant variations in the monthly AMP data reported to CMS for many drugs.[23] Finally, a 2010 report by the Department of Health and Human Services Office of Inspector General (HHS OIG) found significant manufacturer noncompliance with the requirements for reporting AMPs to CMS.[24] In addition, 11 of the 100 drugs in our first basket did not have Part D pricing data for one or more quarters of our analysis period and therefore were removed from the basket when calculating the Part D price indexes to ensure that the same number of drugs were present in each quarter. These 11 drugs represent 8.0 percent of the utilization of this basket.

Our analyses are limited to the commonly used prescription drugs in our basket and cannot be generalized to all prescription drugs. In addition, our U&C analyses are limited to prices reported by retail pharmacies in Pennsylvania to the PACE program and cannot be generalized to all U&C prices nationally for all drugs. We reviewed all data from BCBS FEP, CMS, Red Book, and the PACE program for reasonableness and consistency, including screening for outlier prices and examining possible reasons for inconsistencies between the data sources. We also reviewed documentation and talked to data providers about steps they take to ensure data reliability. We determined that these data were sufficiently reliable for our purposes. We conducted this performance audit from April 2010 through January 2011 in accordance with generally accepted government auditing standards. Those standards require that we plan and perform the audit to obtain sufficient, appropriate evidence to provide a reasonable basis for our findings and conclusions based on our audit objectives. We believe that the evidence obtained provides a reasonable basis for our findings and conclusions based on our audit objectives.

ENCLOSURE II

Drugs Included in Analyses

Table 1 lists the 100 commonly used prescription drugs based on drug name that were used in constructing quarterly price indexes from the first quarter of 2006 through the first quarter of 2010 for our first, second, and third baskets of drugs. Of these 100 drugs used in our first basket, 35 were single-source brand-name drugs throughout our analysis period and 20 additional drugs changed status from single-source to brand-name multisource during our analysis period. Because these two groups of drugs experienced similar price changes, we included both in our second basket of 55 brand-name drugs. Of the remaining 45 commonly used prescription drugs, 40 were generic and 5 were brand-name multisource throughout our analysis period. Because these two groups of drugs experienced similar price changes, we included both in our third basket of 45 generic drugs. Table 2 lists the drugs in our fourth basket of 100 commonly used prescription drugs based on active ingredient that were used in constructing quarterly price indexes that included shifts in BCBS FEP enrollee utilization between brand-name and generic versions of the same drug from the first quarter of 2006 through the first quarter of 2010.

Table 1. The 100 Commonly Used Prescription Drugs Used to Construct Quarterly Price Indexes from 2006 through the First Quarter of 2010, by Drug Name

Drug name, strength, route of administration, and dosage form	Most common 30-day supply
The 55 brand-name drugs	
Aciphex (20mg/oral/tablet, ente)	30
Actonel (35mg/oral/tablet)[a]	4
Advair Diskus 250/50 (0.25mg-0.05m/inhalation/disk)	60
Altace (10mg/oral/capsule)[a]	30
Altace (5mg/oral/capsule)[a]	30
Ambien (10mg/oral/tablet)[a]	30
Aricept (10mg/oral/tablet)	30
Avandia (4mg/oral/tablet)	30
Celebrex (200mg/oral/capsule)	30
Clarinex (5mg/oral/tablet)	30
Cozaar (50mg/oral/tablet)	30
Crestor (10mg/oral/tablet)	30
Detrol LA (4mg/oral/capsule (ER))	30
Diovan (160mg/oral/tablet)	30
Diovan (80mg/oral/tablet)	30
Diovan HCT (12.5mg-160mg/oral/tablet)	30
Effexor-XR(150mg/oral/capsule (ER))	30
Effexor-XR (75mg/oral/capsule (ER))	30
Evista (60mg/oral/tablet)	30
Flomax (0.4mg/oral/capsule)	30
Flonase (0.05mg/actua/nasal/spray)[a]	16
Fosamax (70mg/oral/tablet)[a]	4
Hyzaar (25mg-100mg/oral/tablet)	30
Lantus (100u/1ml/subcutaneous/solution)	10
Lexapro (10mg/oral/tablet)	30
Lexapro (20mg/oral/tablet)	30
Lipitor (10mg/oral/tablet)	30
Lipitor (20mg/oral/tablet)	30
Lipitor (40mg/oral/tablet)	30
Lotrel (5mg-20mg/oral/capsule)[a]	30
Lumigan (0.03%/ophthalmic/solution)	5
Mobic (7.5mg/oral/tablet)[a]	30
Nasonex (0.05mg/actua/nasal/spray)	17

Nexium (40mg/oral/capsule (DR))	30
Niaspan (500mg/oral/tablet (ER))	30
Norvasc (10mg/oral/tablet)[a]	30
Norvasc (5mg/oral/tablet)[a]	30
Plavix (75mg/oral/tablet)	30
Pravachol (40mg/oral/tablet)[a]	30
Premarin (0.625mg/oral/tablet)	30
Prevacid (30mg/oral/capsule (DR))[a]	30
Protonix (40mg/oral/tablet, ente)[a]	30
Singulair (10mg/oral/tablet)	30
Toprol XL (100mg/oral/tablet (ER))[a]	30
Toprol XL (25mg/oral/tablet (ER))[a]	30
Toprol XL (50mg/oral/tablet (ER))[a]	30
Tricor (145mg/oral/tablet)	30
Vytorin (10mg-20mg/oral/tablet)	30
Vytorin (10mg-40mg/oral/tablet)	30
Xalatan (0.005%/ophthalmic/solution)	2
Zetia (10mg/oral/tablet)	30
Zocor (20mg/oral/tablet)[a]	30
Zocor (40mg/oral/tablet)[a]	30
Zoloft (100mg/oral/tablet)[a]	30
Zoloft (50mg/oral/tablet)[a]	30
The 45 generic drugs[b]	
Allopurinol (100mg/oral/tablet)	30
Allopurinol (300mg/oral/tablet)	30
Alprazolam (0.5mg/oral/tablet)	60
Amitriptyline HCL (25mg/oral/tablet)	30
Atenolol (100mg/oral/tablet)	30
Atenolol (25mg/oral/tablet)	30
Atenolol (50mg/oral/tablet)	30
Clonazepam (0.5mg/oral/tablet)	30
Clonazepam (1mg/oral/tablet)	30
Enalapril maleate (20mg/oral/tablet)	30
Fexofenadine HCL (180mg/oral/tablet)	30
Fluoxetine HCL (20mg/oral/capsule)	30
Furosemide (20mg/oral/tablet)	30
Furosemide (40mg/oral/tablet)	30
Gabapentin (300mg/oral/capsule)	90
Glimepiride (4mg/oral/tablet)	30
Glyburide (5mg/oral/tablet)	60
HCTZ/lisinopril (12.5mg-20mg/oral/tablet)	30
HCTZ/triamterene (25mg-37.5mg/oral/capsule)	30
HCTZ/triamterene (37.5mg-25mg/oral/tablet)	30
Hydrochlorothiazide (12.5mg/oral/capsule)	30
Hydrochlorothiazide (25mg/oral/tablet)	30
Isosorbide mononitrate (30mg/oral/tablet (ER))	30

Table 1. (Continued)

Drug name, strength, route of administration, and dosage form	Most common 30-day supply
Klor-Con 10 (10meq/oral/tablet (ER))[c]	30
Klor-Con m20 (20meq/oral/tablet (ER))[c]	30
Levothyroxine sodium (0.05mg/oral/tablet)	30
Lisinopril (10mg/oral/tablet)	30
Lisinopril (20mg/oral/tablet)	30
Lisinopril (40mg/oral/tablet)	30
Lisinopril (5mg/oral/tablet)	30
Lorazepam (1mg/oral/tablet)	30
Metformin HCL (1000mg/oral/tablet)	60
Metformin HCL (500mg/oral/tablet (ER))	60
Metformin HCL (500mg/oral/tablet)	60
Metoprolol tartrate (50mg/oral/tablet)	60
Paroxetine HCL (20mg/oral/tablet)	30
Prednisone (10mg/oral/tablet)	30
Prednisone (5mg/oral/tablet)	30
Ranitidine HCL (150mg/oral/tablet)	60
Spironolactone (25mg/oral/tablet)	30
Synthroid (0.05mg/oral/tablet)[c]	30
Synthroid (0.075mg/oral/tablet)[c]	30
Synthroid (0.1mg/oral/tablet)[c]	30
Trazodone HCL (50mg/oral/tablet)	30
Warfarin sodium (5mg/oral/tablet)	30

Source: GAO analysis of utilization data from the Blue Cross Blue Shield Federal Employee Program, drug status data from the Food and Drug Administration and Red Book, and national drug code data from Red Book.

Notes: Eleven of the 100 drugs had no Medicare Part D data for one or more quarters of our analysis period and were therefore excluded from the calculation of Part D price indexes. These 11 drugs represented 8.0 percent of the total utilization for the basket.

[a] Drug transitioned from single-source to brand-name multisource during our analysis period.

[b] Five of these drugs were brand-name multisource drugs during our entire analysis period. Because these five drugs had generic equivalents available from multiple manufacturers, were marketed under their brand name, and experienced price changes most similar to the 40 generic drugs in our sample, we included them in our third basket of generic drugs.

[c] Drug was brand-name multisource during our entire analysis period.

Table 2. The 100 Commonly Used Prescription Drugs Used in Constructing Quarterly U&C Price Indexes That Included Shifts in Blue Cross Blue Shield Federal Employee Program Enrollee Utilization between Brand-name and Generic Versions of the Drugs from 2006 through the First Quarter of 2010, by Active Ingredient

Active ingredient, strength, route of administration, and dosage form	Most common 30-day supply
Alendronate sodium (70mg/oral/tablet)	4
Allopurinol (300mg/oral/tablet)	30
Alprazolam (0.5mg/oral/tablet)	60
Amlodipine besylate (10mg/oral/tablet)	30
Amlodipine besylate (5mg/oral/tablet)	30
Amlodipine besylate-benazepril hydr (5mg-20mg/oral/capsule)	30
Atenolol (25mg/oral/tablet)	30
Atenolol (50mg/oral/tablet)	30
Atorvastatin calcium (10mg/oral/tablet)	30
Atorvastatin calcium (20mg/oral/tablet)	30
Atorvastatin calcium (40mg/oral/tablet)	30
Bimatoprost (0.03%/ophthalmic/solution)	5
Celecoxib (200mg/oral/capsule)	30
Clonazepam (0.5mg/oral/tablet)	30
Clonazepam (1mg/oral/tablet)	30
Clopidogrel hydrogen sulfate (75mg/oral/tablet)	30
Conjugated estrogens (0.625mg/oral/tablet)	30
Desloratadine (5mg/oral/tablet)	30
Digoxin (0.125mg/oral/tablet)	30
Digoxin (0.25mg/oral/tablet)	30
Diltiazem hydrochloride (240mg/oral/capsule (ER)	30
Enalapril maleate (20mg/oral/tablet)	30
Escitalopram oxalate (10mg/oral/tablet)	30
Escitalopram oxalate (20mg/oral/tablet)	30
Esomeprazole magnesium (40mg/oral/capsule (DR))	30
Ezetimibe (10mg/oral/tablet)	30
Ezetimibe-simvastatin (10mg-20mg/oral/tablet)	30
Ezetimibe-simvastatin (10mg-40mg/oral/tablet)	30
Fenofibrate (145mg/oral/tablet)	30
Fexofenadine hydrochloride (180mg/oral/tablet)	30
Fluoxetine hydrochloride (20mg/oral/capsule)	30

Table 2. (Continued)

Active ingredient, strength, route of administration, and dosage form	Most common 30-day supply
Fluticasone propionate (0.05mg/actua/nasal/spray)	16
Fluticasone propionate-salmeterol x (0.25mg-0.05m/inhalation/disk)	60
Furosemide (20mg/oral/tablet)	30
Furosemide (40mg/oral/tablet)	30
Gabapentin (300mg/oral/capsule)	90
Glimepiride (4mg/oral/tablet)	30
Hydrochlorothiazide (12.5mg/oral/capsule)	30
Hydrochlorothiazide (25mg/oral/tablet)	30
Hydrochlorothiazide-lisinopril (12.5mg-20mg/oral/tablet)	30
Hydrochlorothiazide-losartan potass (25mg-100mg/oral/tablet)	30
Hydrochlorothiazide-triamterene (25mg-37.5mg/oral/capsule)	30
Hydrochlorothiazide-triamterene (25mg-37.5mg/oral/tablet)	30
Hydrochlorothiazide-valsartan (12.5mg-160mg/oral/tablet)	30
Insulin aspart (100u/1ml/subcutaneous/solution)	15
Insulin human glargine (100u/1ml/subcutaneous/solution)	10
Lansoprazole (30mg/oral/capsule (DR))	30
Latanoprost (0.005%/ophthalmic/solution)	2
Levothyroxine sodium (0.025mg/oral/tablet)	30
Levothyroxine sodium (0.05mg/oral/tablet)	30
Levothyroxine sodium (0.075mg/oral/tablet)	30
Levothyroxine sodium (0.088mg/oral/tablet)	30
Levothyroxine sodium (0.125mg/oral/tablet)	30
Levothyroxine sodium (0.15mg/oral/tablet)	30
Levothyroxine sodium (0.1mg/oral/tablet)	30
Lisinopril (10mg/oral/tablet)	30
Lisinopril (20mg/oral/tablet)	30
Lisinopril (40mg/oral/tablet)	30
Lisinopril (5mg/oral/tablet)	30
Lorazepam (1mg/oral/tablet)	30
Losartan potassium (50mg/oral/tablet)	30
Meloxicam (7.5mg/oral/tablet)	30
Metformin hydrochloride (1000mg/oral/tablet)	60
Metformin hydrochloride (500mg/oral/tablet (ER))	60
Metformin hydrochloride (500mg/oral/tablet)	60
Metoprolol succinate (100mg/oral/tablet (ER))	30

Table 2. (Continued)

Active ingredient, strength, route of administration, and dosage form	Most common 30-day supply
Metoprolol succinate (25mg/oral/tablet (ER))	30
Metoprolol succinate (50mg/oral/tablet (ER))	30
Metoprolol tartrate (50mg/oral/tablet)	60
Mometasone furoate (0.05mg/actua/nasal/spray)	17
Montelukast sodium (10mg/oral/tablet)	30
Niacin (500mg/oral/tablet (ER))	30
Pantoprazole sodium (40mg/oral/tablet, ente)	30
Paroxetine hydrochloride (20mg/oral/tablet)	30
Potassium chloride (10meq/oral/tablet (ER))	30
Potassium chloride (20meq/oral/tablet (ER))	30
Pravastatin sodium (40mg/oral/tablet)	30
Prednisone (5mg/oral/tablet)	30
Rabeprazole sodium (20mg/oral/tablet, ente)	30
Raloxifene hydrochloride (60mg/oral/tablet)	30
Ramipril (10mg/oral/capsule)	30
Ramipril (5mg/oral/capsule)	30
Ranitidine hydrochloride (150mg/oral/tablet)	60
Risedronate sodium (35mg/oral/tablet)	4
Rosiglitazone maleate (4mg/oral/tablet)	30
Rosuvastatin calcium (10mg/oral/tablet)	30
Sertraline hydrochloride (100mg/oral/tablet)	30
Sertraline hydrochloride (50mg/oral/tablet)	30
Simvastatin (20mg/oral/tablet)	30
Simvastatin (40mg/oral/tablet)	30
Spironolactone (25mg/oral/tablet)	30
Tamsulosin hydrochloride (0.4mg/oral/capsule)	30
Tolterodine tartrate (4mg/oral/capsule (ER))	30
Trazodone hydrochloride (50mg/oral/tablet)	30
Valsartan (160mg/oral/tablet)	30
Valsartan (80mg/oral/tablet)	30
Venlafaxine hydrochloride (75mg/oral/capsule (ER))	30
Verapamil hydrochloride (240mg/oral/tablet (ER))	30
Warfarin sodium (5mg/oral/tablet)	30
Zolpidem tartrate (10mg/oral/tablet)	30

Source: GAO analysis of utilization data from the Blue Cross Blue Shield Federal Employee Program and national drug code data from Red Book.

ENCLOSURE III

Changes in Drug Price Indexes, 2006 through the First Quarter of 2010

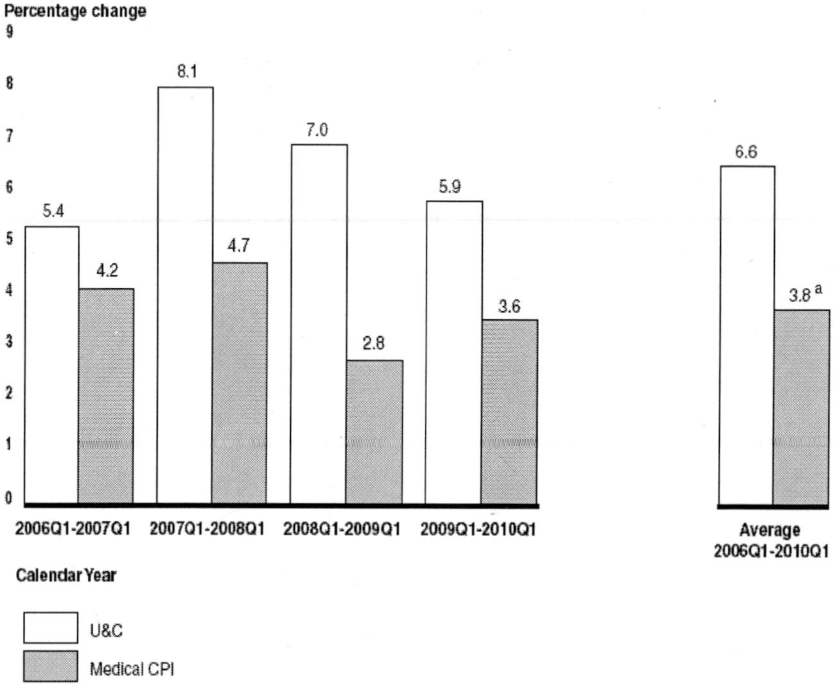

Source: GAO analysis of utilization data from the Blue Cross Blue Shield Federal Employee Program, U&C prices from Pennsylvania's Pharmaceutical Assistance Contract for the Elderly program, and Medical CPI data from the Bureau of Labor Statistics.

[a] The broader CPI-U increased at an average annual rate of 2.2 percent from the first quarter of 2006 through the first quarter of 2010.

Figure 1. Annual Change in the Usual and Customary (U&C) Price Index for a Basket of 100 Commonly Used Prescription Drugs and the Medical CPI, 2006 through the First Quarter of 2010.

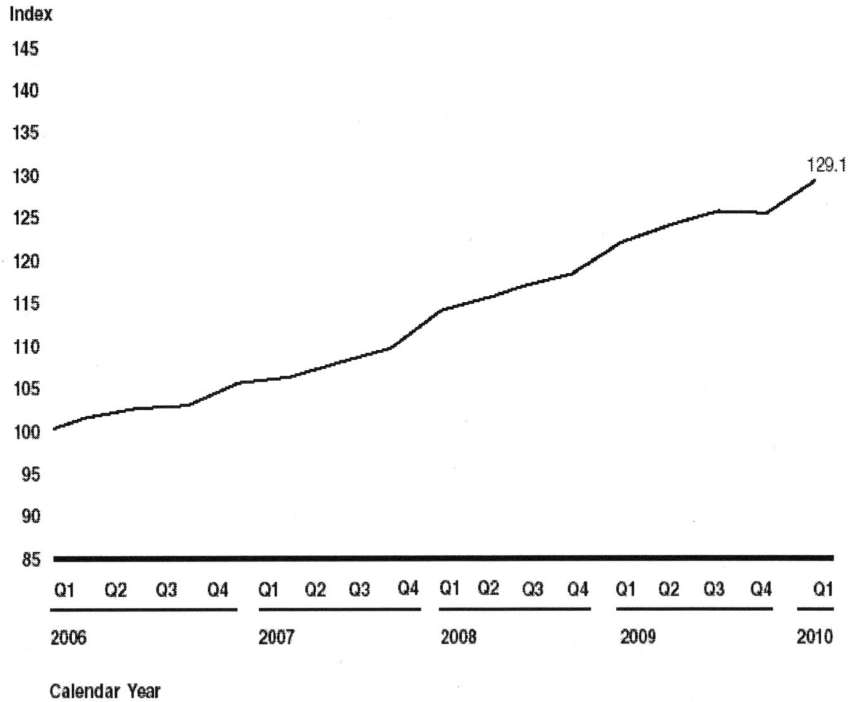

Source: GAO analysis of utilization data from the Blue Cross Blue Shield Federal Employee Progr am and U&C prices from Pennsylvania's Pharmaceutical Assistance Contract for the Elderly progr am.

Note: The index value of 129.1 indicates an increase of 29.1 percent in the average U&C price for the basket of 100 commonly used drugs during our analysis period.

Figure 2. Usual and Customary (U&C) Price Index for a Basket of 100 Commonly Used Prescription Drugs, 2006 through the First Quarter of 2010.

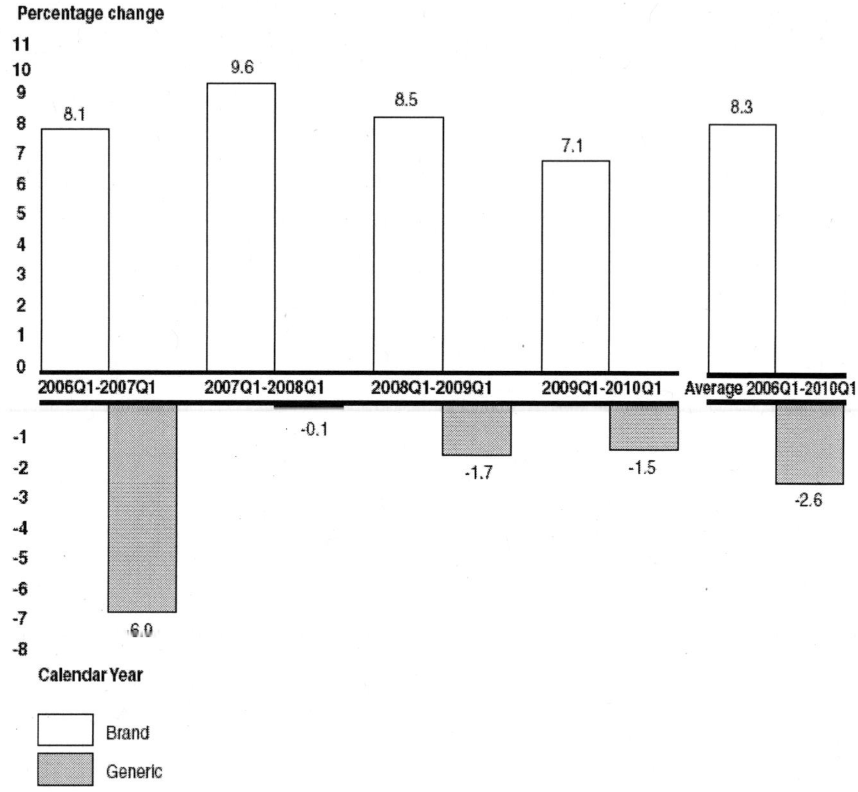

Source: GAO analysis of utilization data from the Blue Cross Blue Shield Federal Employee Program and U&C prices from Pennsylvania's Pha rmaceutical Assista nce Contract for the Elderly program.

Notes: The brand-name drug basket included 35 single-source drugs and 20 drugs that changed from single-source to brand-name multisource during our analysis period. The generic drug basket included 40 generic drugs and 5 brand-name multisource drugs.

Figure 3. Annual Change in the Usual and Customary (U&C) Price Index for a Basket of Commonly Used Brand-name Drugs (55) and Generic Drugs (45), 2006 through the First Quarter of 2010.

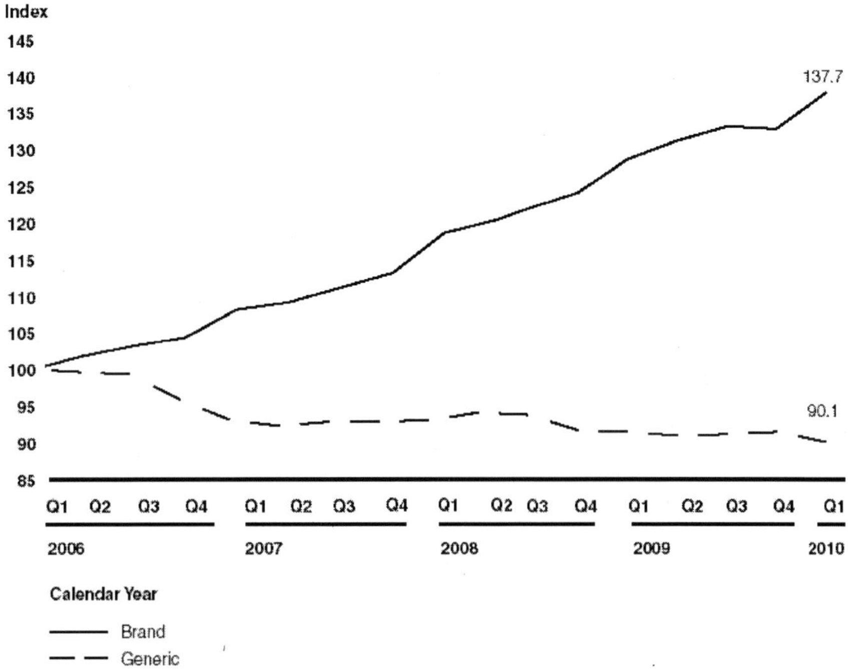

Source: GAO analysis of utilization data from the Blue Cross Blue Shield Federal Employee Program and U&C prices from Pennsylvania's Pharmaceutical Assistance Contract for the Elderly program.

Notes: The brand-name drug basket included 35 single-source drugs and 20 drugs that changed from single-source to brand-name multisource during our analysis period. The generic drug basket included 40 generic drugs and 5 brand-name multisource drugs.

The index value of 137.7 indicates an increase of 37.7 percent in the average U&C price for the basket of 55 commonly used brand-name drugs during our analysis period, and the index value of 90.1 indicates a decrease of 9.9 percent in the average U&C price for the basket of 45 commonly used generic drugs during our analysis period.

Figure 4. Usual and Customary (U&C) Price Indexes for a Basket of Commonly Used Brand-name Drugs (55) and Generic Drugs (45), 2006 through the First Quarter of 2010.

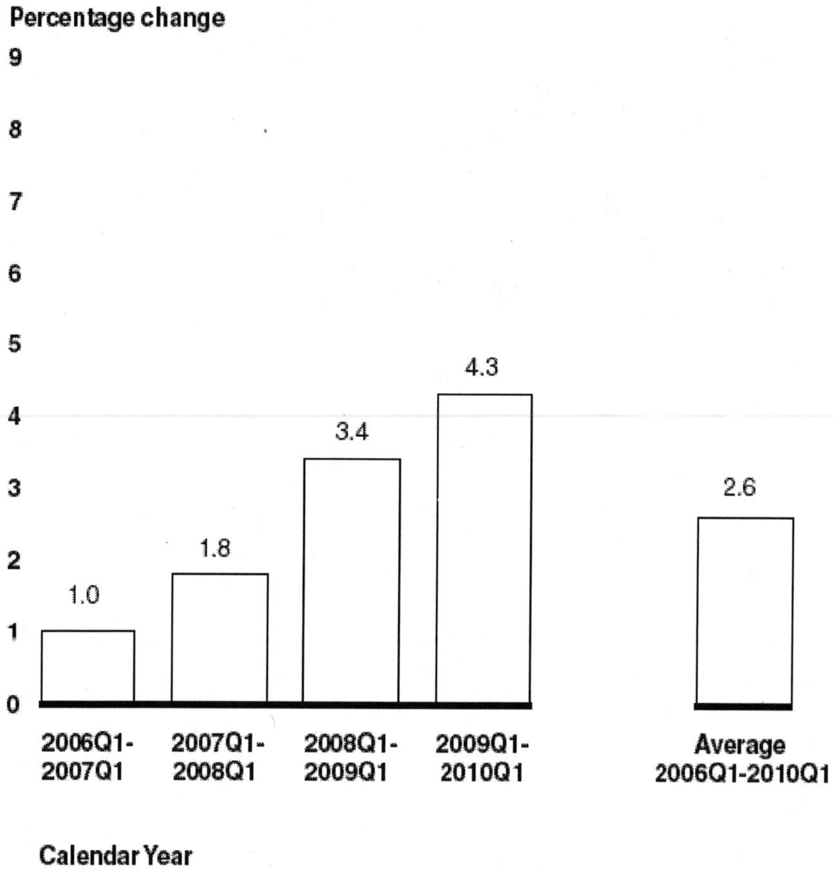

Source: GAO analysis of utilization data from the Blue Cross Blue Shield Feder al Employee Program and U&C prices from Pennsylvania's Pharmaceutical Assistance Contract for the Elderly program.

Figure 5. Annual Change in the Usual and Customary (U&C) Price Index for a Basket of 100 Commonly Used Prescription Drugs When Shifts in Consumer Utilization Between Brand-name and Generic Versions of the Drugs Were Included, 2006 through the First Quarter of 2010.

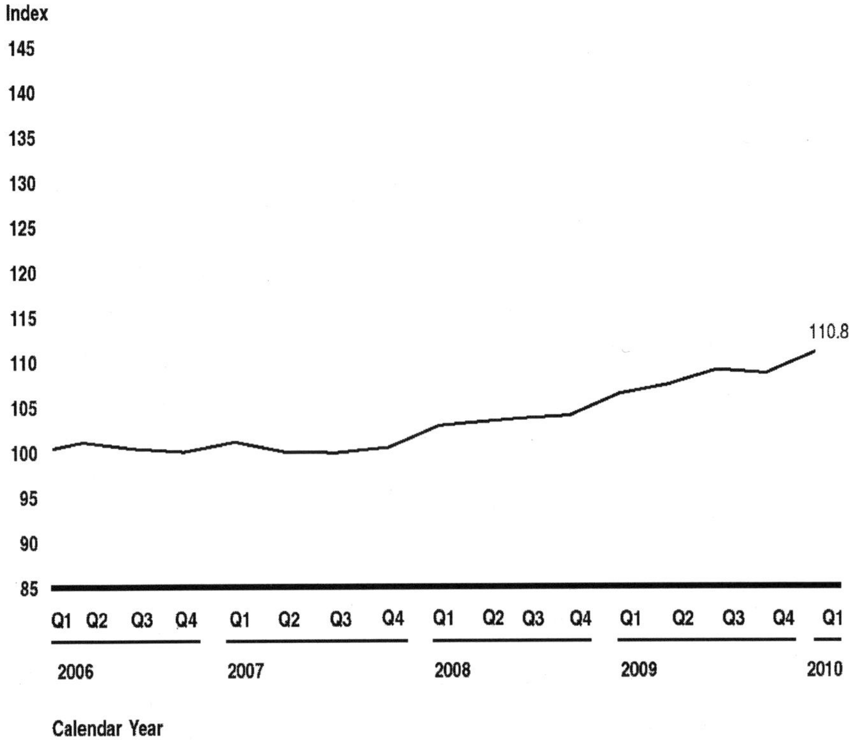

Source: GAO analysis of utilization data from the Blue Cross Blue Shield Feder al Employee Program and U&C prices from Pennsylvania's Pharmaceutical Assistance Contract for the Elderly program.

Note: The index value of 110.8 indicates an increase of 10.8 percent in the average U&C price for a basket of 100 commonly used drugs when shifts in consumer utilization between brand-name and generic versions of the drugs were included.

Figure 6. Usual and Customary (U&C) Price Index for a Basket of 100 Commonly Used Prescription Drugs When Shifts in Consumer Utilization Between Brand-name and Generic Versions of the Drugs Were Included, 2006 through the First Quarter of 2010.

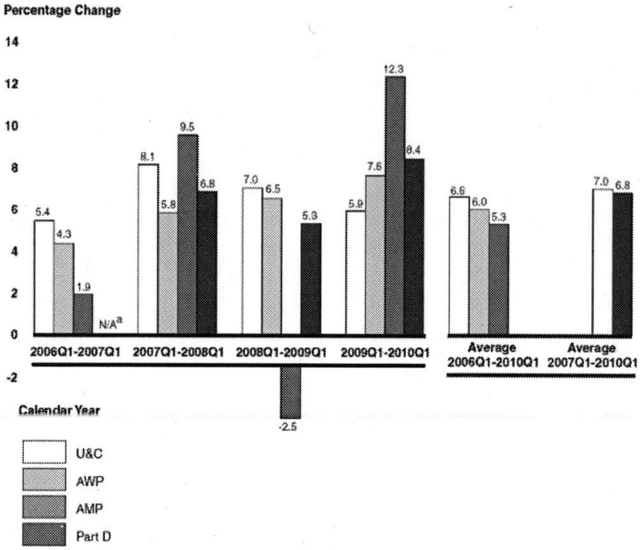

Source: GAO analysis of utilization data from the Blue Cross Blue Shield Federal Employee Program, U&C prices from Pennsylvania's Pharmaceutical Assistance Contract for the Elderly progr am, AWP from Red Book, and AMP and Medicare Part D prices from CMS.

Notes: The AMP price index should be interpreted with caution for several reasons. First, CMS changed the calculation of AMP in accordance with the Deficit Reduction Act of 2005 starting on October 1, 2007 (see footnote 21). In addition, we previously reported significant variations in the monthly AMP data reported to CMS for many drugs (see GAO, *Medicaid Outpatient Prescription Drugs: Second Quarter 2008 Federal Upper Limits for Reimbursement Compared with Average Retail Pharmacy Acquisition Costs*, GAO-10-118R (Washington, D.C.: Nov. 30, 2009)). Finally, a 2010 report by the Department of Health and Human Services Office of Inspector General found significant manufacturer noncompliance with the requirements for reporting AMPs to CMS (see Department of Health and Human Services Office of Inspector General, *Drug Manufacturers' Noncompliance with Average Manufacturer Price Reporting Requirements*, OEI-03-09-00060 (Philadelphia, Pa.: September 2010)).

[a] The Part D price index runs from the first quarter of 2007 through the first quarter of 2010. Of the 100 drugs in our basket, 11T did not have Part D pricing data for one or more quarters of our analysis period and thus were removed from the basket when calculating the Part D price indexes. These 11 drugs represented 8.0 percent of the total utilization for the basket.

Figure 7. Annual Change in the Price Indexes Using Usual and Customary (U&C) and Other Drug Pricing Measures for a Basket of 100 Commonly Used Prescription Drugs, 2006 through the First Quarter of 2010.

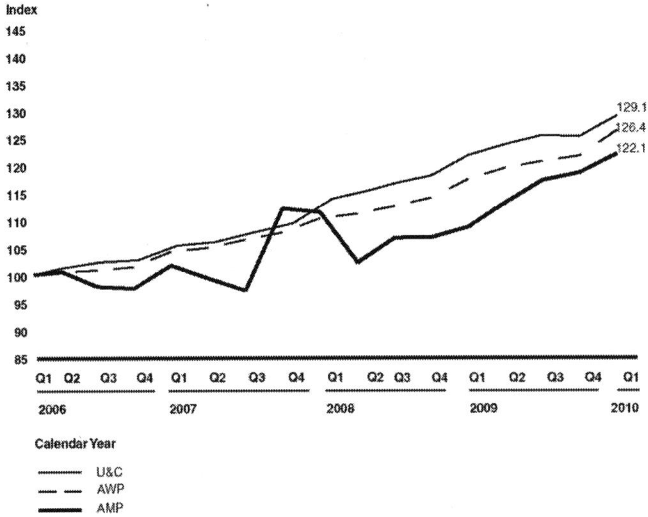

Source: GAO analysis of utilization data from the Blue Cross Blue Shield Federal Employee Program, U&C prices from Pennsylvania's Pharmaceutical Assistance Contract for the Elderly program, AWP from Red Book, and AMP from CMS.

Note: The AMP price index should be interpreted with caution for several reasons. First, CMS changed the calculation of AMP in accordance with the Deficit Reduction Act of 2005 starting on October 1, 2007 (see footnote 21). In addition, we previously reported significant variations in the monthly AMP data reported to CMS for many drugs (see GAO, *Medicaid Outpatient Prescription Drugs: Second Quarter 2008 Federal Upper Limits for Reimbursement Compared with Average Retail Pharmacy Acquisition Costs*, GAO-10-118R (Washington, D.C.: Nov. 30, 2009)). Finally, a 2010 report by the HHS OIG found significant manufacturer noncompliance with the requirements for reporting AMPs to CMS (see Department of Health and Human Services Office of Inspector General, *Drug Manufacturers' Noncompliance with Average Manufacturer Price Reporting Requirements*, OEI-03-09-00060 (Philadelphia, Pa.: September 2010)).

The Part D price index is excluded because Part D data were not available for 2006 or for the fourth quarter of each year.

The index value of 129.1 indicates an increase of 29.1 percent in the average U&C price for the basket of 100 commonly used drugs during the period. The index value of 126.4 indicates an increase of 26.4 percent in the average AWP for the basket of 100 commonly used drugs during the period. The index value of 122.1 indicates an increase of 22.1 percent in the average AMP for the basket of 100 commonly used drugs during our analysis period.

Figure 8. Price Indexes Using Usual and Customary (U&C) and Other Drug Pricing Measures for a Basket of 100 Commonly Used Prescription Drugs, 2006 through the First Quarter of 2010.

ENCLOSURE IV

Percentage Change in Usual and Customary (U&C) Price for 55 Commonly Used Brand-Name Drugs, 2006 through the First Quarter of 2010

Drug name, strength, route of administration, and dosage form	Percentage change in U&C price				
	2006Q1–2007Q1	2007Q1–2008Q1	2008Q1–2009Q1	2009Q1–2010Q1	Average 2006Q1–2010Q1
Flomax (0.4mg/oral/capsule)	9.8	15.1	20.7	24.9	17.6
Ambien (10mg/oral/tablet)	37.5	4.2	11.6	7.7	15.3
Clarinex (5mg/oral/tablet)	20.0	16.3	8.9	4.6	12.5
Premarin (0.625mg/oral/tablet)	12.0	13.2	11.6	11.8	12.2
Altace (5mg/oral/capsule)	6.1	16.7	13.2	10.4	11.6
Altace (10mg/oral/capsule)	6.9	13.7	14.8	10.4	11.5
Effexor-XR (75mg/oral/capsule (ER))	7.9	15.3	6.5	15.1	11.2
Lantus (100u/1ml/ subcutaneous/solution)	12.7	12.4	13.7	5.7	11.1
Lotrel (5mg-20mg/oral/capsule)	9.8	16.2	10.2	8.2	11.1
Effexor-XR (150mg/oral/capsule (ER))	8.9	14.1	5.8	15.1	11.0
Hyzaar (25mg-100mg/oral/tablet)	7.3	11.2	16.6	8.5	10.9
Crestor (10mg/oral/tablet)	5.8	10.7	14.8	12.1	10.9
Aciphex (20mg/oral/tablet, ente)	7.9	7.6	14.0	13.1	10.7
Xalatan (0.005%/ ophthalmic/ solution)	6.5	12.4	14.6	7.8	10.3
Aricept (10mg/oral/tablet)	7.6	10.0	9.6	13.0	10.1
Actonel (35mg/oral/tablet)	8.7	10.3	11.8	6.9	9.4
Diovan (160mg/oral/tablet)	7.5	10.5	10.6	8.0	9.2
Zoloft (50mg/oral/tablet)	8.2	19.9	8.0	-0.2	9.0
Avandia (4mg/oral/tablet)	11.5	3.1	7.6	13.4	8.9
Diovan (80mg/oral/tablet)	6.6	10.6	8.8	9.5	8.9
Vytorin (10mg-40mg/oral/tablet)	11.3	7.8	7.5	8.5	8.8
Diovan HCT (12.5mg-160mg/oral/tablet)	6.6	8.6	11.8	7.6	8.7

Continued

Drug name, strength, route of administration, and dosage form	Percentage change in U&C price				
	2006Q1–2007Q1	2007Q1–2008Q1	2008Q1–2009Q1	2009Q1–2010Q1	Average 2006Q1–2010Q1
Zetia (10mg/oral/tablet)	6.7	13.5	9.0	5.2	8.6
Vytorin (10mg-20mg/oral/tablet)	12.4	6.2	7.1	8.7	8.6
Norvasc (5mg/oral/tablet)	8.5	15.6	6.7	3.4	8.6
Mobic (7.5mg/oral/tablet)	5.3	9.6	14.2	4.8	8.5
Norvasc (10mg/oral/tablet)	8.2	15.1	7.2	3.0	8.4
Advair Diskus 250/50 (0.25mg-0.05m/inhalation/disk)	12.6	7.3	6.5	6.7	8.3
Toprol XL (25mg/oral/tablet (ER))	1.9	13.1	13.1	3.9	8.0
Cozaar (50mg/oral/tablet)	6.3	6.2	10.9	8.6	8.0
Celebrex (200mg/oral/capsule)	6.3	16.9	5.4	3.1	7.9
Protonix (40mg/oral/tablet, ente)	8.5	5.0	6.5	11.4	7.9
Toprol XL (50mg/oral/tablet (ER))	5.4	7.8	11.9	6.2	7.8
Lexapro (20mg/oral/tablet)	9.4	8.9	7.8	5.2	7.8
Lexapro (10mg/oral/tablet)	9.2	8.6	8.7	4.7	7.8
Detrol LA (4mg/oral/capsule (ER))	6.2	14.5	7.0	3.4	7.8
Nasonex (0.05mg/actua/nasal/spray)	8.9	5.5	10.8	5.9	7.8
Toprol XL (100mg/oral/tablet (ER))	5.7	7.8	11.8	5.7	7.8
Singulair (10mg/oral/tablet)	6.6	7.8	9.0	7.2	7.7
Zoloft (100mg/oral/tablet)	5.8	18.8	10.9	-5.5	7.5
Nexium (40mg/oral/capsule (DR))	5.7	9.5	7.9	6.3	7.4
Plavix (75mg/oral/tablet)	2.9	5.2	7.9	12.3	7.1
Niaspan (500mg/oral/tablet (ER))	10.1	6.0	6.6	4.7	6.9
Lumigan (0.03%/ophthalmic/solution)	6.7	9.0	7.6	2.4	6.4
Evista (60mg/oral/tablet)	6.3	7.7	4.4	7.2	6.4
Pravachol (40mg/oral/tablet)	2.1	17.7	5.3	0.3	6.4
Tricor (145mg/oral/tablet)	5.1	5.6	9.0	5.6	6.3
Prevacid (30mg/oral/capsule (DR))	8.2	9.0	4.1	3.5	6.2
Lipitor (10mg/oral/tablet)	6.9	5.9	6.7	5.0	6.1
Lipitor (40mg/oral/tablet)	6.8	5.9	6.5	4.4	5.9

Continued

Drug name, strength, route of administration, and dosage form	Percentage change in U&C price				
	2006Q1–2007Q1	2007Q1–2008Q1	2008Q1–2009Q1	2009Q1–2010Q1	Average 2006Q1–2010Q1
Lipitor (20mg/oral/tablet)	6.5	6.5	6.0	4.2	5.8
Flonase (0.05mg/actua/nasal/spray)	10.2	5.4	1.6	3.2	5.1
Fosamax (70mg/oral/tablet)	6.5	6.6	2.2	3.1	4.6
Zocor (20mg/oral/tablet)	2.5	4.3	3.7	5.6	4.0
Zocor (40mg/oral/tablet)	3.7	1.0	-1.4	5.5	2.2

Source: GAO analysis of utilization data from the Blue Cross Blue Shield Federal Employee Program and U&C prices from Pennsylvania's Pharmaceutical Assistance Contract for the Elderly program.

End Notes

[1] *NHE Web Tables*, National Health Expenditures data for 2009 (the most recent available at the time of our analysis), http://www.cms.gov/nationalhealthexpenddata/02_nationalhealth accountshistorical.asp (accessed Jan. 20, 2011).

[2] The U&C price is the price an individual without prescription drug coverage would pay at a retail pharmacy.

[3] See GAO, *Prescription Drugs: Trends in Usual and Customary Prices for Drugs Frequently Used by Medicare and Non-Medicare Health Insurance Enrollees,* GAO-07-1201R (Washington, D.C.: Sept. 7, 2007). For additional GAO reports on drug pricing, see *Prescription Drugs: Trends in Usual and Customary Prices for Drugs Frequently Used by Medicare and Non-Medicare Enrollees,* GAO-05-104R (Washington, D.C.: Oct. 6, 2004) and *Prescription Drugs: Price Trends for Frequently Used Brand and Generic Drugs from 2000 through 2004*, GAO-05-779 (Washington, D.C.: Aug. 15, 2005).

[4] See Duff Wilson, "Drug Makers Raise Prices in Face of Health Care Reform," *The New York Times*, Nov. 16, 2009 and Emily Brandon, "Drug Prices Outpace Inflation," *US News*, Nov.17, 2009.

[5] Pub. L. No. 111-148, 124 Stat. 119 (2010).

[6] In selecting our four baskets of drugs, we excluded drugs with fewer than 10 claims in Pennsylvania's Pharmaceutical Assistance Contract for the Elderly program and drugs with zero BCBS FEP claims in one or more of the quarters to assure the drugs were commonly used and continuously marketed throughout our analysis period.

[7] For example, all claims for "Zocor/10mg/oral/tablet" were combined as one drug. Using this approach, the brand-name and generic versions of a drug were aggregated separately. For example, "Zocor/10mg/oral/tablet" and "simvastatin/10mg/oral/tablet" would be considered different drugs for purposes of our first basket because they have different names, even though they are the brand-name and generic versions of drugs containing the same active ingredient.

[8] Five of these drugs were brand-name multisource drugs that had generic equivalents available from multiple manufacturers and were marketed under their brand name during our entire

analysis period. These 5 brand-name multisource drugs experienced price changes most similar to the 40 generic drugs in our sample and were therefore included in our third basket of generic drugs.

[9] For example, all claims with "simvastatin" as the active ingredient and "10mg/oral/tablet" as the strength, route, and dosage form were combined as one drug. Using this approach, the brand-name and generic versions of a drug were combined as one drug. For example, "Zocor/10mg/oral/tablet" and "simvastatin/10mg/oral/tablet" would be considered the same drug for purposes of this fourth basket because they are the brand-name and generic versions of the same drug, even though they have different names.

[10] We compared our price indexes to both the medical CPI and the CPI-U because the CPI-U, which describes price changes across a wide range of consumer goods and services, may not appropriately reflect price changes that occur within the health care industry—particularly during the recent economic downturn—and therefore may not provide appropriate context for increases in drug prices. Prescription drugs account for about 18.8 percent of the medical CPI and about 1.2 percent of the CPI-U.

[11] The Part D price index runs from the first quarter of 2007 through the first quarter of 2010. We used the first quarter of 2007 as the baseline when calculating the Part D price index because reliable Part D data for 2006 were not available; fourth quarter data for each year were also not available. In addition, 11 of the 100 drugs in our first basket did not have Part D pricing data for one or more quarters of our analysis period and therefore were removed from the basket when calculating the Part D price indexes. These 11 drugs represented 8.0 percent of the total utilization of the basket.

[12] Red Book is a drug pricing compendium with information about prices and other characteristics of drug products, published by Thomson Reuters.

[13] The broader CPI-U increased at an average annual rate of 2.2 percent from 2006 through the first quarter of 2010.

[14] For all drugs selected for our baskets, we obtained corresponding 11-digit national drug codes (NDCs) from Red Book. NDCs are three-segment numbers that are the universal product identifiers for drugs for human use. The Food and Drug Administration assigns the first segment of the NDC, which identifies the firm that manufactures, repackages, or distributes a drug. The second segment identifies a specific strength, dosage form, and formulation for a particular firm. The third segment identifies the package size and type. A drug can have multiple NDCs associated with it. For example, a drug made by one manufacturer, in one strength or dosage form, but in three package sizes would have three NDCs.

[15] In selecting our four baskets, we excluded any drug that had zero BCBS FEP claims in one or more quarters of our analysis period—first quarter 2006 through first quarter 2010—and any drugs that had fewer than 10 claims in Pennsylvania's Pharmaceutical Assistance Contract for the Elderly program in one or more of the quarters to assure the drugs were commonly used and continuously marketed throughout our analysis period.

[16] Red Book is a drug pricing compendium with information about prices and other characteristics of drug products, published by Thomson Reuters.

[17] Single-source drugs include those brand-name drugs that have no generic equivalent on the market and are generally available from only one manufacturer. Brand-name multisource drugs include those brand-name drugs that have generic equivalents available from multiple manufacturers and are marketed under their brand names.

[18] Generic drugs include multisource drugs that have the same active ingredient as their branded counterparts and are generally marketed by multiple manufacturers under a nonproprietary name.

[19] We removed PACE claims for which the U&C drug price fell outside two standard deviations from the mean price per 30-day supply for each quarter.

[20] We compared our price indexes to both the medical CPI and the CPI-U because the CPI-U, which describes price changes across a wide range of consumer goods and services, may not appropriately reflect price changes that occur within the health care industry—

particularly during the recent economic downturn—and therefore may not provide appropriate context for increases in drug prices. Prescription drugs are responsible for about 18.8 percent of the medical CPI and about 1.2 percent of the CPI-U.

[21] The Medicare Prescription Drug Plan Finder data were provided by a CMS contractor as average, utilization-weighted negotiated prices across all plans for each drug under Medicare Part D as reported to CMS by Part D plan sponsors. The data did not include non-Part D plans; national Program of All-Inclusive Care for the Elderly plans; employer sponsored plans; demonstration plans; or plans whose pharmacy data were suppressed in the Public Use File reporting period because of plan request, data inaccuracy, or other issues identified by CMS. The contractor considered the 2006 data unreliable and was not able to provide pricing data for the fourth quarter of any year in our analysis period because of the way those data are reported. Medicare Part D Plan Finder data are based on proxy NDCs and do not include data for all NDCs. A unique proxy NDC is assigned by CMS to each drug at the brand name, generic name, dosage form, and strength level. CMS recommends that this same proxy NDC be used for all therapeutically equivalent versions of a drug. Therefore, we applied the prices for proxy NDCs to all NDCs associated with the same name, strength, and dosage form when calculating the Part D price indexes.

[22] The AMP definition was amended again with the enactment of PPACA. We did not factor this change into our analysis because the analysis included data only through the end of the first quarter of 2010, prior to the effective date of the pertinent changes made by PPACA. See Pub. L. No. 111-148, § 2503(a)(2), d, 124 Stat. 119, 310-12 (2010), as amended by the Health Care and Education Reconciliation Act of 2010 (HCERA), Pub. L. No. 111-152, § 1101(c), 124 Stat. 1029, 1039 and Pub. L. No. 111-226, § 202, 124 Stat. 2389, 2394 (2010); Pub. L. No. 109-171, § 6001(c), 120 Stat. 4, 54-6 (2006); 72 Fed. Reg. 39142 (July 17, 2007).

[23] See GAO, *Medicaid Outpatient Prescription Drugs: Second Quarter 2008 Federal Upper Limits for Reimbursement Compared with Average Retail Pharmacy Acquisition Costs,* GAO-10-118R (Washington, D.C.: Nov. 30, 2009).

[24] See Department of Health and Human Services Office of Inspector General, *Drug Manufacturers' Noncompliance with Average Manufacturer Price Reporting Requirements,* OEI-03-09-00060 (Philadelphia, Pa.: September 2010).

In: Prescription Drug Pricing
Editors: J. R. Dickson, A. M. Woebler
ISBN: 978-1-61324-639-9

Chapter 2

Lack of Therapeutically Equivalent Drugs and Limited Competition May Contribute to Extraordinary Price Increases

United States Government Accountability Office

Why GAO Did This Study

The growing cost of brand-name prescription drugs—FDA-approved drug products that typically have patent protection—is a concern for patients, payers, and providers of health care—particularly when price increases are large and occur suddenly. A 2008 congressional hearing by the Joint Economic Committee drew attention to some small market prescription drugs that had an extraordinary price increase—a price increase of 100 percent or more at a single point in time.

GAO was asked to examine extraordinary price increases for brand-name prescription drugs. Specifically, GAO examined the: (1) frequency of extraordinary price increases for brand-name prescription drugs from 2000 to 2008, (2) characteristics of the brand-name prescription drugs that had extraordinary price increases, and (3) factors that contributed to the extraordinary price increases experienced by these brand-name prescription drugs. To determine the frequency and characteristics of the brand-name prescription drugs that experienced an extraordinary price increase, GAO reviewed drug pricing and other data from a pharmaceutical industry compendium. To illustrate the factors that may contribute to extraordinary price increases, GAO developed case studies of six brand-name prescription drugs identified from the analysis of drug pricing data. These brand-name prescription drugs were selected based on factors including price, and the percentage and number of price increases.

WHAT GAO FOUND

From 2000 to 2008, 416 brand-name drug products—different drug strengths and dosage forms of the same drug brands—had extraordinary price increases. These 416 brand-name drug products represented 321 different drug brands. The number of brand-name drug products that had these extraordinary price increases represents half of 1 percent of all brand-name drug products. The number of extraordinary price increases each year more than doubled from 2000 to 2008 and most of the extraordinary price increases ranged between 100 percent and 499 percent. Almost 90 percent of all brand-name drug products that had an extraordinary price increase sustained the new higher price—by either having another increase in price or remaining at the increased price.

More than half of the brand-name drug products that had extraordinary price increases were in just three therapeutic classes—central nervous system, anti-infective, and cardiovascular. These therapeutic classes include drugs used to treat conditions such as fungal or viral infections, and heart disease. About half of the extraordinary price increases were for brand-name drug products that were purchased from drug manufacturers or wholesalers, repackaged, and resold in smaller packages to health care providers such as hospitals or physicians. However, some drug repackagers serve a niche in the drug market, and therefore may have a small share of the market in a therapeutic class. The majority of all extraordinary price increases were for drugs priced less than $25 per unit; however, a full course of treatment for some of these drugs could total several thousand dollars.

Based on interviews with experts and industry representatives, a lack of therapeutically equivalent drugs—both generics and other brand-name drugs used to treat the same condition—and limited competition may contribute to extraordinary price increases. The limited availability of therapeutically equivalent drugs may result from patent protection and market exclusivity, and the size of the market for a given drug. Patent protection and market exclusivity temporarily limit competition and thereby allow a drug company to recoup research and development costs and earn a return on its financial investment. Two of six case study drugs that had extraordinary price increases were patented at the time of the extraordinary price increase. The transfer of the rights to a drug and corporate consolidations among drug companies may result in fewer drug options and contribute to extraordinary price increases, according to experts. For example, the rights to four of the case-study drugs were obtained by a new drug company, and two of these drugs had an extraordinary price increase shortly after the rights to the drugs were purchased. Finally, experts and industry representatives noted that unusual events—such as disruptions in production due to shortages of raw materials—and other factors, including manufacturing issues, may also contribute to some extraordinary price increases.

ABBREVIATIONS

AWP	average wholesale price
DOJ	Department of Justice
FDA	Food and Drug Administration
FTC	Federal Trade Commission
NDC	national drug code

December 22, 2009

The Honorable Charles E. Schumer
Vice Chairman
Joint Economic Committee
United States Congress

The Honorable Amy Klobuchar
United States Senate

The growing cost of brand-name prescription drugs can be a burden on patients, payers, and providers of health care—particularly when price increases are large and occur suddenly. Controlling rising prescription drug prices helps to ensure that patients can afford medically necessary and sometimes life-saving medications, and to moderate costs for hospitals and third-party payers such as insurance plans and state and federal governments.

However, a hearing held in July 2008 by the Joint Economic Committee drew attention to certain prescription drugs that recently had an extraordinary price increase—a price increase equal to 100 percent or more at a single point in time.

Drug manufacturers may consider several factors when setting prices for brand-name prescription drugs, including a drug's patent status and market exclusivity. Patents and market exclusivity may provide a limited period of protection from competition, thereby allowing a drug company to recoup research and development costs and earn a return on its financial investment. Drug manufacturers may obtain patents or patent extensions from the U.S. Patent and Trademark Office. In addition, independent of a drug product's patent status, the Federal Food, Drug, and Cosmetic Act authorizes various periods of market exclusivity for drug products.

In this report, GAO studied extraordinary price increases for brand-name prescription drugs. Specifically, we examined (1) the frequency of extraordinary price increases for brand-name prescription drugs from 2000 to 2008, (2) the characteristics of the brand-name prescription drugs that had extraordinary price increases, and (3) the factors that contributed to the extraordinary price increases experienced by these brand-name prescription drugs.

To determine the frequency of extraordinary price increases, we reviewed the average wholesale price (AWP)[1] for all brand-name prescription drugs in Thomson Reuters' Red Book,[2] and identified all extraordinary price increases—a unit price[3] increase of 100 percent or more at a single point in time—from 2000 to 2008. Red Book includes drug prices for each package size (for example, 30, 60, or 100 tablets) and dosage form (for example, tablet or injection) of a brand-name drug.[4] We report the frequency of extraordinary price increases in two ways—by drug brand (or drug label name as recorded in Red Book) and by brand-name drug product. For the drug brand frequencies, we counted an extraordinary price increase if the price of any version of a brand-name drug increased by 100 percent or more at a single point in time. For brand-name drug products, we counted each extraordinary price increase for each version—drug strength and dosage form—of the brand-name drug separately. For example, if both the 1mg and 5mg tablet versions of a drug had extraordinary price increases, we categorized this as one drug brand increase, and as two brand-name drug product increases (one for each version of the brand-name drug). The frequencies of extraordinary price increases reported include brand-name drug products that were repackaged for resale to health care providers such as hospitals or physicians.[5] To identify the characteristics of brand-name drug products that had an extraordinary price increase, we used Red Book data on therapeutic class[6] and price.

To identify the factors that may contribute to extraordinary price increases, we interviewed drug policy experts; academic researchers; state and federal government officials; consumer advocates; insurance company representatives; and representatives from hospital, health insurance, and retail pharmacy associations. To illustrate the factors that may contribute to extraordinary price increases, we developed case studies of six different brand-name drugs from different drug companies identified from our analysis of Red Book data. Each brand-name drug that was active in the market as of December 31, 2008 and that had an extraordinary price increase was eligible for selection for the case study. To achieve variability in the characteristics of the brand-name drugs reviewed for the case study, our selection was based on several factors, including a drug's price, the level of the percentage increase, whether the drug had more than one extraordinary price increase between 2000 and 2008, availability of the drug from multiple sources, and permanence of the price increase. To gain an understanding of the market and other dynamics leading to the extraordinary price increase experienced by each brand-name drug in our case studies, we interviewed representatives of the companies that manufacture and distribute these brand-name drugs,[7] and obtained information about each drug company's business strategy from the companies' Web sites, annual and quarterly reports, and other resources. (See app. I for a detailed description of our scope and methodology.)

We reviewed the Red Book data file to assess its reliability. This review involved an assessment of the variables in Red Book to identify incorrect and erroneous entries or extreme outliers. We compared a random sample of the pricing data reported in Red Book with pricing data in another drug pricing compendium. Based on this review, we determined that the data used in this report were adequate for our purposes.

We conducted our work from October 2008 through December 2009 in accordance with all sections of GAO's Quality Assurance Framework that are relevant to our objectives. The framework requires that we plan and perform our engagement to obtain sufficient and appropriate evidence to meet our stated objectives and to discuss any limitations in our work. We believe that the information and data obtained, and the analysis conducted, provide a reasonable basis for any findings and conclusions in this product.

BACKGROUND

Extraordinary price increases for brand-name drugs can lead to substantially higher drug spending for public and private insurance plans, hospitals, and other providers that cover prescription drugs. Patients may also face higher out-of-pocket costs and reduced access to medically necessary and sometimes life-saving drugs. In addition, extraordinary price increases for brand-name drugs may contribute to overall drug spending, which has increased an average of about 10 percent a year since 2000.[8] As reported during the Joint Economic Committee hearing, a small but growing subset of drugs have had very large and sudden price increases since 2000, raising questions about the competitiveness of the prescription drug marketplace.

Overview of Brand-name Drugs

Brand-name drugs are drug products that have received FDA approval and typically have patent protection.[9] After the patent and any applicable period of market exclusivity expires, these drugs are still considered brand-name drugs, but other drug companies may develop a generic equivalent—a similar drug that contains the same active ingredient, strength, dosage form, route of administration, and intended use.[10] The FDA reviews and approves both brand-name and generic prescription drugs.

Brand-name drugs may be supplied to health care providers from companies other than a drug's manufacturer. For example, brand-name drugs may be repackaged from large drug inventories into smaller packages, and sold by a repackaging company using a unique national drug code (NDC). Repackagers include health maintenance organizations, pharmacies, and private companies. Repackagers are required to follow FDA guidelines, such as registering annually with the FDA and labeling drugs under the same brand name. Repackagers may obtain prescription drugs from wholesalers, and sell the repackaged drugs to health care providers such as hospitals or physicians who then dispense them to patients. Proponents of repackaged drugs believe that they offer convenience to patients and may reduce medication errors.[11] However, some experts suggest that repackaging drugs may unnecessarily increase drug prices and profits. Repackagers may assign AWPs for repackaged drugs that differ from the AWP suggested by the drug's manufacturer.

Patents, Market Exclusivity, and Orphan Drugs

Patents and market exclusivity protect prescription drugs by limiting competition for a set period of time. A drug manufacturer may seek a 20-year patent on various aspects of its new chemical entity from the U.S. Patent and Trademark Office.[12] Once a patent is granted, other drug manufacturers are excluded from making, using, or selling the patented formula during the life of the patent. Companies that develop new brand-name drugs generally obtain a patent on the active ingredient used in the drug. Patents may be granted for other properties of a brand-name drug, such as its formulation and composition, and/or method of use.[13] After receiving a patent on a brand-name drug, drug companies typically seek approval from the FDA for use of the drug to treat certain indications.

Market exclusivity may be granted for approved drugs and is independent of the rights granted by a patent. The Federal Food, Drug, and Cosmetics Act authorizes various periods of market exclusivity for drug products. Generally, market exclusivities prevent the FDA from approving any application for a competing drug compound for a stated period of time. These exclusivities may relate to new chemical entities (5 years),[14] previously approved drugs with a new application that is based on new clinical studies (3 years),[15] generic drugs (180 days),[16] drugs tested for use in children (6 months),[17] and orphan drugs (7 years).[18] Market exclusivity and patent protection may run concurrently.

The Joint Economic Committee hearing in July 2008 identified certain brand-name drugs which treat rare diseases that experienced extraordinary price increases. Incentives are available for drug companies to develop innovative drugs for rare diseases (orphan drugs). In addition to the 7-year market exclusivity status, these incentives may include tax incentives of up to 50 percent of the cost of clinical research, and a waiver of FDA fees.[19] Research grants are also available through the FDA for the development of drugs used to treat rare diseases or conditions.

Drug Market Trends

According to experts, the drug industry's traditional business model is changing. In the past, large drug companies conducted research and development on several drugs, with the goal of releasing one or more "blockbuster" drugs that treat a large population and can earn billions of dollars. Recently, drug companies have increasingly focused on specialty drugs that target niche markets, or a smaller population of people with a narrow indication or medical condition. According to experts and industry representatives, the pace of consolidation among drug companies through mergers and acquisitions and transfers of drug ownership rights has increased. Fewer companies producing and marketing drugs can lead to greater market domination among certain companies and less competition. In addition, large drug companies have purchased other drug companies that specialize in manufacturing drugs targeting niche populations or drugs in similar therapeutic classes.

Setting Prescription Drug Prices

According to some economists, the usual mechanisms that enforce market discipline may not work in the same manner in the health care market. In most markets—automobiles, for example—consumers are expected to be conscious of the price of goods. If a company raises the price of its goods, consumers would likely purchase fewer goods, causing the company's revenues to decline. However, health care providers influence demand because they typically act on behalf of patients, who may remain unaware of drug costs. If the patient is insured and their medical bills are paid by a third-party payer, then demand may not be significantly influenced by changes in price to the extent that it might be in other markets. Some price restraint may be provided by pharmacy benefit managers and health plans that use drug formularies to negotiate price rebates on brand name prescription drugs.

According to industry representatives and experts, drug companies may consider several issues when setting the price of a drug. These include: (1) the perceived value of a drug relative to its competitors, such as its ease of use; (2) the unique characteristics of a drug, such as its novelty, the frequency of administration, and safety; (3) the cost of therapeutically alternative drugs and alternative therapies, such as surgery, medical devices, and existing drugs; (4) the disease treated; (5) the size and characteristics of the patient market; (6) research and development, manufacturing, and marketing costs; (7) the willingness of customers to pay for the drug; and (8) the amount of reimbursement for the drug from third-party payers. To mitigate high drug prices some companies subsidize the price of some of their brand-name drugs through a patient assistance program to low-income uninsured or underinsured patients.[20]

Federal Oversight

While prescription drug pricing in the private sector is not subject to federal regulation, drug companies are subject to antitrust enforcement. The Federal Trade Commission (FTC) and the U.S. Department of Justice (DOJ) enforce federal antitrust laws that prohibit activities such as mergers and acquisitions that may substantially reduce competition or create a monopoly.[21] Companies are required to notify the FTC and DOJ of certain pending mergers, also known as the pre-merger notification program.[22] In addition, the FTC has authority to investigate and take action against unfair methods of competition affecting commerce, including in the drug industry.[23] Price fixing agreements between businesses, certain monopolies, and other anticompetitive conduct are subject to review and enforcement action. FTC officials indicated that the FTC has not brought a case against a drug company for charging extraordinarily high prices because such activity is not expressly prohibited by federal law, and because high drug prices in the absence of anticompetitive behavior are not per se illegal. The FTC has challenged anticompetitive patent settlements between brand-name and generic drug manufacturers. For example, FTC officials indicated that the agency has filed cases challenging "pay-to-delay" settlements in which a brand-name manufacturer shares a portion of its future profits with a potential generic competitor in exchange for an agreement to delay marketing the generic prescription drug.

Finally, drugs must be manufactured in accordance with FDA regulations called good manufacturing practices, and the FDA inspects manufacturing facilities before a drug can be approved.[24] Good manufacturing practices are designed to ensure the safety and quality of drug products and lay out minimum standards for the facilities and equipment used in manufacturing drug products. All drug manufacturers—including companies that acquire the rights to a drug from another manufacturer—are required to comply with good manufacturing practices.

More Than 400 Extraordinary Price Increases Occurred for Over 300 Drug Brands from 2000 to 2008

Between 2000 and 2008, 416 brand-name drug products representing 321 drug brands had extraordinary price increases. Most often, these extraordinary price increases ranged from 100 percent to 499 percent, but in a few cases were 1,000 percent or more.

From 2000 to 2008, 416 Extraordinary Price Increases Occurred for 321 Different Drug Brands

From 2000 to 2008, 416 brand-name drug products representing 321 drug brands had an extraordinary price increase. A number of these 321 drug brands had two or more extraordinary price increases between 2000 and 2008. The number of brand-name drug products that had these extraordinary price increases each year trended upwards, more than doubling from 2000 to 2008; however, they represent about half of 1 percent of all brand-name drug products. (See table 1 for the frequency of extraordinary price increases.) Most brand-name drug products that had an extraordinary price increase sustained the new price after the extraordinary price increase occurred.[25] For example, following the extraordinary price increase, about 87 percent of the brand-name drug products remained at the increased price, or had another increase in price, and only 13 percent had a decrease in price.[26]

A number of these brand-name drug products had more than one extraordinary price increase. For example, 21 of the 416 brand-name drug products had more than one extraordinary price increase between 2000 and 2008, and 9 of those 21 brand-name drug products had more than one extraordinary price increase in the same year. The 416 brand-name drug products were sold by 91 drug companies, and 12 of these 91 drug companies sold brand-name drug products that had more than one extraordinary price increase between 2000 and 2008. Furthermore, 4 of these 91 drug companies sold brand-name drug products that had more than one extraordinary price increase within the same year. (See app. II for a list of brand-name drugs that had an extraordinary price increase.)

While Most Extraordinary Price Increases Were Less Than 500 Percent, Some Increases Were 1,000 Percent or More

Most extraordinary price increases—for 357 of the 416 brand-name drug products with extraordinary price increases—ranged from 100 percent to 499 percent.[27] Overall, the median increase for brand name drug products was about 158 percent. However, some brand-name drug products had very large extraordinary price increases. For example, 26 brand-name drug products had extraordinary price increases greater than 1,000 percent—a tenfold increase. The largest extraordinary price increase for brand-name drug products was about 4,200 percent. (See table 2 for the frequency of extraordinary price increases by percent increase.) In addition, 7 brand-name drug products had extraordinary price increases of 500 percent or more multiple times from 2000 to 2008.

MOST BRAND-NAME DRUG PRODUCTS WITH EXTRAORDINARY PRICE INCREASES WERE IN THREE THERAPEUTIC CLASSES, COST LESS THAN $25 PER UNIT, OR WERE REPACKAGED

Brand-name drug products that had extraordinary price increases shared similar characteristics including therapeutic class, cost, or packaging. While extraordinary price increases occurred in 20 therapeutic classes, more than half of the increases fell into 3 therapeutic classes—central nervous system agents, anti-infective agents, and cardiovascular agents. Most extraordinary price increases were for brand-name drug products costing less than $25 per unit. Depending on the condition treated and length of treatment, the full cost of treatment for a drug could total several thousand dollars. More than half of all extraordinary price increases were for repackaged brand-name drug products.

Three Therapeutic Classes Accounted for More Than Half of the Extraordinary Price Increases

While extraordinary price increases for brand-name drug products occurred in 20 therapeutic classes, the majority of the drugs— 52 percent— that had extraordinary price increases fell into 3 therapeutic classes—central nervous system, anti-infective, and cardiovascular drugs.[28]

Table 1. Annual Frequency of Extraordinary Price Increases for Brand-name Drugs, 2000 to 2008

Category	2000	2001	2002	2003	2004	2005	2006	2007	2008	Total
Drug brands[a]										
Number of extraordinary price increases for drug brands	24	21	23	38	38	33	38	52	54	**321**
Brand-name drug products[b]										
Number of extraordinary price increases for brand-name drug products	28	27	31	48	51	39	47	74	71	**416**
Total number of all brand-name drug products on the market[c]	**11,503**	**11,503**	**11,106**	**11,413**	**11,436**	**11,979**	**12,798**	**12,895**	**13,193**	**N/A**[d]

Source: GAO analysis of average wholesale price from Red Book.

Note: Drug prices are identified and reported by a unique national drug code (NDC).

[a] A drug brand is the drug label name as recorded in Red Book.

[b] A brand-name drug product includes the same drug brand with different strengths and dosage forms. The frequencies for brand-name drug products are reported using NDC-9s.

[c] Total number of brand-name drugs recorded in the Red Book for each calendar year. As of December 31, 2008, some of these drugs were no longer active on the market.

[d] Totals for the period are not provided. Drugs that were recorded in Red Book may appear in multiple years.

Table 2. Annual Frequency of Extraordinary Price Increases for Brand-name Drug Products by Percentage Increase in Price, 2000 to 2008

Category	2000	2001	2002	2003	2004	2005	2006	2007	2008	Total
Brand-name drug products[a]										
Total brand-name drug products with extraordinary increase in price	**28**	**27**	**31**	**48**	**51**	**39**	**47**	**74**	**71**	**416**
100-499 percent	22	15	23	43	43	37	43	64	67	**357**
500-999 percent	3	3	6	5	6	2	2	3	3	**33**
1,000-1,499 percent	0	4	0	0	2	0	1	2	1	**10**
1,500-1,999 percent	1	3	0	0	0	0	0	3	0	**7**
More than 2,000 percent	2	2	2	0	0	0	1	2	0	**9**

Source: GAO analysis of average wholesale price from Red Book.

Note: Drug prices are identified and reported by a unique NDC.

[a] A brand-name drug product includes the same drug brand with different strengths and dosage forms. The frequencies for brand-name drug products are reported using NDC-9s.

Table 3. Therapeutic Classes of Brand-name Drug Products That Had Extraordinary Price Increases, 2000 to 2008

Therapeutic class	2000	2001	2002	2003	2004	2005	2006	2007	2008	Total
Brand-name drug products[a]										
Central nervous system agents	9	6	6	16	12	13	20	24	20	**126**
Anti-infective agents	9	2	9	8	8	6	6	2	5	**55**
Cardiovascular agents	3	2	1	0	4	4	5	5	11	**35**

Table 3. (Continued)

Therapeutic class	2000	2001	2002	2003	2004	2005	2006	2007	2008	Total
Other therapeutic classes	7	15	15	23	27	16	16	42	31	**192**
Total brand-name drug products that increased in price[b]	**28**	**27**	**31**	**48**	**51**	**39**	**47**	**74**	**71**	**416**

Source: GAO analysis of average wholesale price from Red Book.

Note: Drug prices are identified and reported by a unique NDC.

[a]A brand-name drug product includes the same drug brand with different strengths and dosage forms. The frequencies for brand-name drug products are reported using NDC-9s.

[b]Columns do not add up to total because eight records were not classified into a therapeutic class in Red Book.

Table 4. Frequency of Extraordinary Price Increase by Price Level, by Brand-name Drug Products, 2000 to 2008

Price prior to increase	100-499 percent	500-999 percent	1,000-1,499 percent	1,500-1,999 percent	2,000 percent or more	Total
Brand-name drug products[a]						
Less than $25.00 per unit	344	31	8	7	9	**399**
$25.00 to $49.99 per unit	4	0	1	0	0	**5**
$50.00 or more per unit	9	2	1	0	0	**12**
Total number of brand-name drug products that increased in price	**357**	**33**	**10**	**7**	**9**	**416**

Source: GAO analysis of average wholesale price from Red Book.

Note: Drug prices are identified and reported by a unique NDC.

[a] A brand-name drug product includes the same drug brand with different strengths and dosage forms. The frequencies for brand-name drug products are reported using NDC-9s.

- Central nervous system—126 brand-name drug products had extraordinary price increases. Central nervous system drugs include sedatives and antidepressants, and are typically used to treat depression or anxiety.
- Anti-infective—55 brand-name drug products had extraordinary price increases. Anti-infective drugs are used to treat infections caused by fungi, bacteria, or viruses.
- Cardiovascular drugs—35 brand-name drug products had extraordinary price increases. Cardiovascular drugs such as anti-arrhythmia agents are used to treat the heart.

The remaining 17 therapeutic classes comprised 192 brand-name drug products that had extraordinary price increases. (See table 3 for frequency of extraordinary price increases by therapeutic class.)

Brand-name Drug Products Priced Less Than $25 Per Unit Accounted for Most of the Extraordinary Price Increases

Ninety-six percent of brand-name drug products that had extraordinary price increases cost less than $25 per unit prior to the price increase.[29,30] Overall, brand-name drug products that had an extraordinary price increase ranged in price from $0.01 per unit to $5,400 per unit prior to the price increase. The median price of the brand-name drug products that had an extraordinary price increase rose from $1.66 per unit before the increase to $4.70 per unit after the increase.[31] (See table 4 for the frequency of extraordinary price increases by price level.)

It is important to note that the unit price of a drug is only one factor in determining the cost of a full course of treatment for a medical condition. Other factors affecting cost include the total number of units prescribed and the duration of the treatment. For example, the full cost of treatment for a drug that is priced less than $25 per unit could total several thousand dollars or more. One of the drugs we reviewed that is used to treat a rare cancer cost $390 for a full course of treatment prior to the extraordinary price increase.[32] After two extraordinary price increases, the full cost of a course of treatment rose to more than $3,000.

Table 5. Annual Frequency of Extraordinary Price Increases for Repackaged and Nonrepackaged Brand-name Drug Products, 2000 to 2008

Category	2000	2001	2002	2003	2004	2005	2006	2007	2008	Total
Brand-name drug products[a]										
Repackaged drugs that increased in price	18	10	15	27	19	29	33	31	29	**211**
Nonrepackaged drugs that increased in price	10	17	16	21	32	10	14	43	42	**205**
Total brand-name drugs that increased in price	28	27	31	48	51	39	47	74	71	**416**
Total number of all repackaged brand-name drug products on the market[b]	**3,162**	**3,496**	**3,307**	**3,648**	**3,743**	**4,333**	**5,078**	**5,423**	**5,690**	**N/A**[c]

Source: GAO analysis of average wholesale price from Red Book.

Note: Drug prices are identified and reported by a unique NDC.

[a] A brand-name drug product includes the same drug brand with different strengths and dosage forms. The frequencies for brand-name drug products are reported using NDC-9s.

[b] Total number of brand-name drugs recorded in Red Book for each calendar year. As of December 31, 2008, some of these drugs were no longer active on the market.

[c] Totals for the period are not provided. Drugs that were recorded in Red Book may appear in multiple years.

Repackaged Drugs Accounted for More Than Half of the Extraordinary Price Increases for Brand-name Drug Products

More than half of the brand-name drug products that had extraordinary price increases were repackaged—that is, purchased from drug manufacturers or wholesalers and resold in smaller packages to health care providers such as hospitals or physicians.[33] (See table 5 for frequency of extraordinary price increases for repackaged and nonrepackaged drugs.) Almost all the extraordinary price increases for repackaged drugs appear to have originated from the company that repackaged the drug rather than from the company that manufactured the drug.[34] Specifically, 95 percent of repackaged drugs had an extraordinary price increase without a corresponding extraordinary price increase by the drug's manufacturer for the identical nonrepackaged drug. However, some drug repackagers serve a niche in the drug market and therefore may have a small share of the market in a therapeutic class.

Almost one-fifth of the 91 companies that sold brand-name drug products that had extraordinary price increases were repackagers. The four companies with the greatest number of brand-name drug products that had an extraordinary price increase were repackagers—ranging from 26 to 51 brand-name drug products per repackaging company.[35] About 99 percent of repackaged drugs cost less than $25 per unit.[36] The median price of repackaged drugs that had extraordinary price increases rose from $2.14 per unit to $5.39 per unit after the increase.[37]

Lack of Therapeutically Equivalent Drugs and Limited Competition May Contribute to Extraordinary Price Increases for Brand-name Drugs

Based on interviews with experts and industry representatives, we found that a lack of therapeutically equivalent drugs—generics and other brand-name drugs used to treat the same condition—and limited competition may contribute to extraordinary price increases. According to these experts and industry representatives, the availability of few therapeutically equivalent drugs may result from patent protection and market exclusivity, and the limited size of the market for a given drug. Experts noted that the transfer of drug rights and corporate consolidations may limit competition among drug companies, resulting in few drug options. The experts and industry representatives also noted that unusual events—such as disruptions in production due to shortages of raw materials—and other factors may also contribute to some extraordinary price increases.

Limited Availability of Therapeutic Equivalents: Experts we interviewed said that drugs without therapeutic equivalents—in some cases due to patents or a limited market size—may be more likely to have an extraordinary price increase.[38] Experts and industry representatives also reported that competition within a therapeutic class of drugs may be limited by (1) patents for a new drug, such as patents for the active ingredient; (2) patents for existing drugs that have been modified by, for example, changing a drug's active ingredient, strength, or delivery mechanism;[39] and (3) market exclusivity protections. Patents and market exclusivity may limit the entry of other prescription drugs into the market. An expert also noted that no single factor leads to extraordinary price increases, rather a combination of several factors likely contributes to these extraordinary price increases.

Two of our six case study drugs[40] had patent protection at the time of the extraordinary price increase. (See app. III for a summary of the characteristics of the case study drugs.) One drug had a method-of-use patent and was the only FDA-approved drug available to treat an acute illness affecting infants and young children. The other drug was under patent at the time of its extraordinary price increase, and was sold by a licensed repackager that purchased the drug from wholesalers.

In addition, experts and industry representatives we interviewed reported that small market drugs, such as orphan drugs or drugs for rare diseases, may lack therapeutically equivalent drugs, and thus may be prone to extraordinary price increases. When the target patient population or market for a drug is relatively small, there may be little financial incentive for potential competitors to enter the market and offer competing drugs. Two of the drugs we examined in our case studies treat rare diseases. These drugs did not have generic equivalents at the time of their extraordinary price increases; however, the drug companies reported the availability of other drugs that treat similar conditions. Both drugs had more than one extraordinary price increase—one of the drugs had two price increases that were each more than 1,000 percent, and the other had extraordinary price increases in 2 consecutive years.

Representatives of the manufacturer for one of these drugs reported that their company's business model is based almost solely on sales from the drug that had the extraordinary price increases. This drug is currently approved for several dozen indications, and the company is funding research on other uses for the drug. The second company reported that its business model is structured around facilitating the development of drug products for rare diseases. The company provides financial support to researchers developing new drugs for rare diseases and obtains the rights to the drugs created by these researchers. The company considered their financial support for developing other rare disease drugs when determining the price of their drug. Furthermore, a representative of this company stated that it had obtained other drugs that were discontinued by a prior owner and then reintroduced the drugs onto the market. Both of these drug companies market specialized drugs that treat rare diseases.

Transfer of Drug Rights, Corporate Consolidations, Mergers, and Acquisitions: Experts and industry representatives we interviewed reported that transfers of drug ownership rights and consolidations among drug companies have increased.[41] These transfers and consolidations may limit competition as companies that may offer competing prescription drugs in a therapeutic class merge or sell their rights to a drug, potentially leading to extraordinary price increases for drugs. Fewer drug companies competing in a therapeutic class may lead to fewer prescription drugs being developed and sold within that class. Industry representatives and experts reported that larger drug companies are acquiring drugs from smaller drug companies that conduct drug research. Notwithstanding potential FTC or DOJ review, drug companies may still acquire competitors that offer similar drugs, potentially leading to market domination in a therapeutic class.[42] The rights to four of our case study drugs were obtained by a new drug company, and two of these drugs had an extraordinary price increase shortly after the rights to the drugs were purchased.

Unusual Events: Extraordinary price increases were also attributed by industry representatives and experts to the occurrence of unusual events, such as disruptions in the production of a drug due to shortages of necessary raw materials or the added costs to renovate outdated drug production plants. For example, a drug in our case study was purchased from a drug company that was suspending production of the drug. The company that purchased this drug reported investing millions of dollars transferring and upgrading the manufacturing equipment, processes, and testing methods required to make the drug. The drug's manufacturer attributed the first of two extraordinary price increases to compensating for the drug's production expenses and other costs.

Prior to the company's purchase of the drug, it was sold only in limited quantities through a patient advocacy group.[43] Another drug from our case study was purchased by a company that spent several years trying to identify a technical partner capable of processing the drug's active ingredient, which was difficult to manufacture because of its cytotoxic nature and the limited quantity of drugs produced. The company's representative stated that due to the unique challenges of producing the active ingredient of the drug, two companies were involved in manufacturing and packaging the drug. As a result of changes made in manufacturing the drug, the company reported investing several million dollars upgrading its manufacturing equipment and processes in order to meet updated FDA regulations.[44] This company considered its investment to produce a stable supply of the drug when pricing the product.

Other Factors: Representatives of the drug companies we reviewed for our case studies reported that they considered other factors when determining the price of their drugs. For example, one expert noted that extraordinary price increases may occur because a drug manufacturer updates the price of a drug after obtaining new information about certain demand and supply factors affecting the drug. Three of the drug companies reported that their products were difficult to manufacture. These companies employ third-party manufacturers that produce the drugs. One of these companies said that its drug was very toxic, and since its manufacturing equipment was used to make other drug products, the equipment must be decontaminated after each batch is produced. These drug companies factored in these additional costs when they raised the price of their products.

Some of the drug companies we reviewed revised the price of their brand-name drugs to bring them in line with the prices of what they regarded as similar drugs. One company reviewed the estimated annual cost of several orphan drugs when determining the price for its drug, which treats a rare disease. Three companies reviewed various drug products and priced their drugs in line with these drugs. This pricing strategy led, in part, to these drugs experiencing an extraordinary price increase. An official from one of these companies reported that the drug was underpriced, and the company increased the price of the drug based on the prices of competing drug products used for similar medical conditions. Some of the drug companies considered the financial solvency of their drug product and company, and their fiduciary responsibility to their shareholders when determining the price of their drug.

In some cases, representatives of drug companies cited the quantity of free or low-cost drugs donated through their patient assistance program and the level of rebates paid to the Medicaid program as factors that they considered when raising the price of their brand-name drugs.[45] Two drug companies said that the level of rebates paid to the Medicaid program was a factor for their drugs' extraordinary price increases.[46] The companies reported that they charged a higher retail price for their drugs, in part, to account for the large financial outlays to patient assistance and government programs. One company said that Medicaid beneficiaries represent a large portion of the patient population that uses their drug product. This company's representatives stated that over half of its drug sales were targeted to their patient assistance program for low-income, underinsured, or uninsured individuals or were reimbursed under Medicaid and therefore subject to rebates. These companies reported that they offered patient assistance programs that provide a large volume of free prescription drugs to patients who meet established criteria. The programs also provide financial assistance to insured patients who face financial hardship from paying copayments or coinsurance.

Expert Comments

We provided a draft of this report to drug policy experts, who provided technical comments that we incorporated as appropriate.

As agreed with your offices, unless you publicly announce the contents of this report earlier, we plan no further distribution until 30 days from the report date. At that time, we will send copies of this report to other interested parties. We will also provide copies to others upon request. In addition, the report is available at no charge on the GAO Web site at http://www.gao.gov.

If you or your staff have any questions about this report, please contact me at (202) 512-7114 or at dickenj@gao.gov. Contact points for our Offices of Congressional Relations and Public Affairs can be found on the last page of this report. GAO staff members who made major contributions to this report are listed in appendix IV.

John E. Dicken
Director, Health Care

APPENDIX I. SCOPE AND METHODOLOGY

In this report we address the following objectives: (1) the frequency of extraordinary price increases for brand-name prescription[47] drugs from 2000 to 2008, (2) the characteristics of the brand-name drugs that had extraordinary price increases, and (3) the factors that contributed to the extraordinary price increases experienced by these brand-name drugs.

To determine the frequency of extraordinary price increases, we reviewed the average wholesale price (AWP)[48] for all brand-name drugs in Thomson Reuters' Red Book,[49] and identified all extraordinary price increases—a unit price increase[50] equal to 100 percent or more at a single point in time from 2000 to 2008. We calculated the percent change in unit AWP recorded in the Red Book for each 11-digit national drug code (NDC-11).[51] For example, where a NDC-11 had three unit prices reported in Red Book from 2000 to 2008 (unit price at point 1, unit price at point 2, and unit price at point 3), two data records were created. One record contained the percent change in unit price from point 1 to point 2, and the other record contained the percent change from point 2 to point 3. We identified extraordinary price increases by selecting only records (NDC-11s) with a percent change of 100 percent or more.

Drugs sold in different package sizes—for example, 30, 60, or 100 tablets—have different NDC-11 codes. Each NDC-11 record captures the label name of the drug which includes the dosage form of the drug. Because a brand-name drug may have several NDC-11 codes for different package sizes, we identified the number of brand-name drug products that had an extraordinary price increase by their NDC-9 code, which represents the manufacturer and drug name, and strength. Where more than one package size of the same brand-name drug had an extraordinary price increase, we selected the package size with the highest extraordinary price increase.[52] We counted an NDC-9 with different package sizes that had an extraordinary price increase on the same date only once. In this report, we use three terms to refer to the brand-name prescription drugs recorded in the Red Book. Drug brand refers to the label name of a brand-name prescription drug; brand-name drug product refers to the different products of the same drug brand. Otherwise we use the term brand-name drug or drug when we do not need to distinguish between drug brand and brand-name drug product. We report the frequency of brand-name drugs that had extraordinary price increases by (1) drug brand (drug label name as recorded in Red Book), and (2) brand-name drug product (NDC-9 code). The frequencies of extraordinary price increases reported by brand-name drug products (NDC-9) include the same drug brand sold in different strengths and dosage forms (e.g., a 1mg or a 5mg tablet). The frequency of extraordinary price increases reported includes brand-name drug products that were repackaged by a distributor for resale to health care providers.[53,54] (See app. II for a list of the brand-name drugs that had extraordinary price increases.) To identify the characteristics of brand-name drugs that had an extraordinary price increase, we used Red Book data on therapeutic class and price.

To identify the factors that may contribute to extraordinary price increases we interviewed drug policy experts; academic researchers; state and federal government officials; consumer advocates; insurance company representatives; and hospital, health insurance, and retail pharmacy associations representatives. To illustrate the factors that may contribute to extraordinary price increases, we developed case studies of six drugs from different companies identified from our analysis of Red Book data. Each brand-name drug (NDC-11) was eligible for inclusion as a case study if it was active in the market as of December 31, 2008, and had an extraordinary price increase. To achieve variability in the characteristics of the drugs reviewed for the case study, selection was based on several factors, such as the (1) unit price, (2) percentage increase in price, (3) year of increase, (4) number of increases, (5) availability from multiple sources, (6) orphan drug status, and (7) permanence of the price increase.

We also interviewed representatives of the companies that manufactured and distributed the case study drugs about the market dynamics leading to the drugs' extraordinary price increases. We gathered information on: (1) the characteristics of each drug, such as its patent and market exclusivity status, indication, volume, and utilization; (2) corporate business and marketing strategy for each drug; (3) factors that influenced the extraordinary price increase; and (4) agreements with the makers of drugs in the same therapeutic class. Some information provided by the representatives during these interviews is considered proprietary. As a result, the names of the participating companies and brand-name drugs are not identified. (See app. III for information on each of the drugs from the case studies.) Information was also obtained from drug companies' Web sites, annual and quarterly reports, and other resources.

We systematically reviewed Red Book to assess its reliability. The review involved an assessment of the frequencies of all numeric and date variables in Red Book to identify incorrect and erroneous entries or extreme outliers.[55] We compared a sample of the pricing data for brand-name drugs that had extraordinary price increases reported in Red Book with pricing data contained in another drug pricing compendium and found a high degree of concurrence between the prices recorded in both data sources. Based on this review, we determined that the data used in our report were adequate for our purposes. We conducted our work from October 2008 through December 2009 in accordance with all sections of GAO's Quality Assurance Framework that are relevant to our objectives. The framework requires that we plan and perform our engagement to obtain sufficient and appropriate evidence to meet our stated objectives and to discuss any limitations in our work. We believe that the information and data obtained, and the analysis conducted, provide a reasonable basis for any findings and conclusions in this product.

APPENDIX II. BRAND-NAME PRESCRIPTION DRUGS WITH AN EXTRAORDINARY PRICE INCREASE, 2000 TO 2008

Using Thomson Reuters' Red Book,[56] we calculated the change in average wholesale price (AWP) and identified all unit price increases equal to 100 percent or more at a single point in time from 2000 to 2008. (See app. I for more information.) Based on this analysis, we identified the label names of drugs that had extraordinary price increases by their NDC-9 code.[57] AWP records in Red Book are reported by the drug manufacturer and published in Red Book. In some cases, when drug manufacturers do not report AWP, Red Book calculates AWP from other drug pricing benchmarks provided by drug manufacturers. GAO did not audit the drug pricing information reported to Red Book by drug manufacturers nor the calculations performed by Red Book to fill nonreported AWP data. Some of the drugs on this list were repackaged, or nonrepackaged, while other drugs were both repackaged and nonrepackaged. In a few cases, drugs were removed from the list because changes in the recorded package size led to errors in the calculated change in unit prices. See table 6 below for the label names of brand-name prescription drugs that had an extraordinary price increase between 2000 and 2008.

Table 6. Repackaged Brand-name Drug Products that Had an Extraordinary Price Increase, 2000 to 2008

Repackaged brand name drugs (Pricing for these drugs is typically set by the repackager and not the drug's manufacturer)		
Name and strength of drug	**Name and strength of drug**	**Name and strength of drug**
Abilify Tab 5MG	Floxin Tab 300MG	Provera Tab 2.5MG
Actos Tab 15MG	Floxin Tab 400MG	Prozac Cap 20MG
Actos Tab 30MG	Fulvicin P/G Tab 330MG	Restoril Cap 30MG
Adderall Tab 5MG	Glyset Tab 25MG	Risperdal Tab 1MG
Ambien Tab 5MG	Ionamin Cap 15MG	Risperdal Tab 0.5MG
Ambien Tab 10MG	Ismo Tab 20MG	Risperdal Tab 0.25MG
Amoxil Cap 250MG	Lamictal Tab 25MG	Robinul Inj 0.2MG/ML
Amoxil Cap 500MG	Lamictal Tab 200MG	Septra DS Tab
Anaprox Tab 275MG	Lanoxin Tab 0.25MG	Seroquel Tab 25MG
Anaprox-DS Tab 550MG	Levaquin Tab 250MG	Seroquel Tab 100MG
Ansaid Tab 100MG	Levaquin Tab 500MG	Seroquel Tab 50MG
Antabuse Tab 250MG	Levaquin Leva-pak 750MG	Silvadene Cre 1%
Aricept Tab 10MG	Levoxyl Tab 0.088MG	Singulair Tab 10MG
Arthrotec Tab 75MG-0.2MG	Lidoderm Patch 5%	Skelaxin Tab 400MG
Avandia Tab 4MG	Lipitor Tab 80MG	Skelaxin Tab 800MG
Axert Tab 12.5MG	Locoid Cre 0.1%	Soma Compound w/Code Tab
Bayhep B Inj	Lomotil Tab 0.025MG-2.5MG	Sumycin Cap 250MG
Bextra Tab 20MG	Lotensin Tab 40MG	Synalgos-DC Cap
Biaxin Sus 250MG/5ML	Lunesta Tab 1MG	Synthroid Tab 0.1MG
Bontril Cap ER 105MG	Lunesta Tab 2MG	Synthroid Tab 0.088MG
Bontril Slow Cap 105MG	Lunesta Tab 3MG	Terazol 3 Vag Cre 0.8%
Brevital Sodium Inj 500MG	Lyrica Cap 100MG	Tigan Inj 100MG/ML

Table 6. (Continued)

Repackaged brand name drugs (Pricing for these drugs is typically set by the repackager and not the drug's manufacturer)		
Name and strength of drug	**Name and strength of drug**	**Name and strength of drug**
Bromfed Tab	Lyrica Cap 200MG	Tobradex Opth Sus
Cataflam Tab 50MG	Lyrica Cap 50MG	Tobrex Opth Sol 0.3%
Ceftin Tab 125MG	Lyrica Cap 75MG	Topamax Tab 25MG
Ceftin Tab 250MG	Marcaine Inj 0.5%	Topamax Tab 100MG
Ceftin Tab 500MG	Maxitrol Opth Sus	Toprol XL Tab 50MG
Celebrex Cap 200MG	Mephyton Tab 5MG	Transderm Scop Patch
Celebrex Cap 100MG	Methergine Tab 0.2MG	Ultram Tab 50MG
Cerumenex Otic Sol 10%	Mevacor Tab 20MG	Ultram ER Tab ER 200MG
Cipro Tab 500MG	Miacalcin Spr 200iu/Act	Valium Tab 5MG
Cipro Tab 750MG	Miralax Pwd for Soln	Valtrex Tab 1GM
Claritin Tab 10MG	Mobic Tab 15MG	Vicodin Tab
Codiclear DH Syr	Mobic Tab 7.5MG	Vicoprofen Tab
Combivir Tab	Motrin Tab 800MG	Vioxx Tab 25MG
Compazine Sup 25MG	Niferex-150 Forte Cap	Viracept Tab 250MG
Compazine Tab 10MG	Nitrolingu Spr 0.4/Spray	Viramune Tab 200MG
Coumadin Tab 2.5MG	Nitrostat SL Tab 0.4MG	Vivelle-Dot 0.1MG/24hrs
Cutivate Cre 0.05%	Norco Tab	Voltaren Tab 75MG
Cytotec Tab 200mcg	Norflex Tab 100MG	Zebeta Tab 5mg
Dalmane Cap 30MG	Norvasc Tab 10MG	Ziagen Tab 300MG
Daypro Tab 600MG	Norvir Cap 100MG	Zithromax Tab 250MG
Depo-Estradio Inj 5MG/ML	Ovral Tab	Zithromax Z-Pak Tab 250MG
Desowen CRE 0.05%	Paxil CR Tab 25MG	Zocor Tab 10MG
Diovan Tab 160MG	Paxil CR Tab 12.5MG	Zocor Tab 20MG

Table 6. (Continued)

Repackaged brand name drugs (Pricing for these drugs is typically set by the repackager and not the drug's manufacturer)		
Name and strength of drug	**Name and strength of drug**	**Name and strength of drug**
Dovonex Cre 0.005%	Paxil CR Tab 37.5MG	Zocor Tab 40MG
Dovonex Oin 0.005%	Pediazole Sus	Zoloft Tab 25MG
Duricef Cap 500MG	Pepcid Tab 40MG	Zyprexa Tab 10MG
E.E.S.-400 Film Tab 400MG	Peridex Liq 0.12%	Zyprexa Tab 2.5MG
Econopred Plus OP Sus 1%	Phenergan Tab 25MG	Zyprexa Tab 7.5MG
Effexor Tab 100MG	Phenergan Sup 12.5MG	Zyprexa Tab 5MG
Effexor XR Cap ER 75MG	Phenergan Sup 50MG	
Effexor-XR Cap 75MG	Phenhist Expectorant Liq	
Effexor-XR Cap 37.5MG	Phoslo Tab 667MG	
Eryc Cap 250MG	Plendil Tab 5MG	
Estrace Tab 1MG	Plendil Tab 10MG	
Flexeril Tab 5MG	Ponstel Cap 250MG	
Flovent Inh 0.22/Act	Premarin Tab 0.625MG	
Floxin Tab 200MG	Prilosec Cap 20MG	

Source: GAO analysis of Red Book data.

Note: Following the extraordinary price increase, some drugs may have become discontinued or transferred from one manufacturer to another. In some cases, an extraordinary price increase for a drug may not be attributed to the manufacturer that currently owns the drug.

Table 7. Nonrepackaged Brand-name Drug Products that Had an Extraordinary Price Increase, 2000 to 2008

Nonrepackaged brand name drugs		
Name and strength of drug	**Name and strength of drug**	**Name and strength of drug**
Adderall Tab 5MG	Hectorol Cap 2.5MCG	Omnipaque 300 Inj 64.7%
Ala-Scalp HP Lot 2%	Hectorol Liq Cap 2.5MCG	Oncoscint CR/OV Inj 1MG
Amytal Sodium Inj 0.5GM	Hep-Lock Inj 10U/ML	Optison IV Susp
Ancobon Cap 250MG	Histatrol Inj 0.275/ML	Oracit Sol
Ancobon Cap 500MG	Histatrol Soln 2.75MG/ML	Ortho-Prefest Tab
Bensal HP 60MG-30MG/1GM	Histussin HC 2.5-5-1/5	Pamelor Cap 10MG
Bontril PDM Tab 35MG	Hypaque-76 Inj	Pamelor Cap 25MG
Bontril Slow Cap ER 105MG	Inderal LA Cap 60MG	Panhematin IV 313MG
Brethine Inj 1MG/ML	Inderal LA Cap 80MG	Phrenilin Forte 50-650
Brevital Sodium 2.5GM	Inderal LA Cap 120MG	Prefest Tab
Brevital Sodium Inj 2.5GM	Inderal LA Cap 160MG	Prevacid SoluTab 15MG
Buprenex Inj 0.3MG/ML	Inderal LA Cap ER 120MG	Prevacid SoluTab 30MG
Capital w/Codeine Sus	Inderal LA Cap ER 160MG	Prevpac Kit
Cefazolin 1GM/50ML	Inderal LA Cap ER 60MG	Promit IV 150MG/1ML
Cefotan Inj 1GM	Inderal LA Cap ER 80MG	Quelicin Inj 100MG/ML
Cefotan Inj 2GM	Indocin IV Pwd for Soln	Quelicin Inj 20MG/1ML
Cellcept Cap 250MG	Indocin Susp 25MG/5ML	Regonol Inj Soln 5MG/1ML
Cenolate Inj 500MG/ML	Infumorph 200 Inj	Rejuvesol Inj
Ceretec Kit	Infumorph 500 Inj	Rescon-MX Tab ER
Cogentin Inj Soln 1MG/1ML	Inversine Tab 2.5MG	Robaxin Inj Soln 100MG/ML
Cognex Cap 10MG	Iodopen Inj 118MCG/1ML	Robinul Inj Soln 0.2MG/ML

Table 7. (Continued)

Nonrepackaged brand name drugs		
Name and strength of drug	**Name and strength of drug**	**Name and strength of drug**
Cognex Cap 20MG	Isuprel Inj 0.2MG/ML	Roxicet Tab 500MG-5MG
Cognex Cap 30MG	Kenalog Spr 0.147/GM	Ryna-12 S Sus
Cognex Cap 40MG	Lacrisert Opth Dev 5MG	Seconal Sodium Cap 100MG
Combipatch 0.05MG-0.14MG	Levo-Dromoran Tab 2MG	Septra DS Tab
Combipatch 0.05MG-0.25MG	Liposyn III Inj 10%	Sucraid Sol 8500 IU/ML
Cortrosyn Inj 0.25MG	Liposyn III Inj 20%	Sulfoxyl Regular Lot
Cosmegen IV 0.5MG	Liposyn III IV Emul 10%	Sulfoxyl Strong Lot
Cuprimine Cap 250MG	Liposyn III IV Emul 20%	Sumycin Tab 250MG
Cystadane 1GM/1Scoopful	Locoid Oin 0.1%	Sumycin Tab 500MG
D.H.E. 45 Inj 1MG/ML	Locoid Sol 0.1%	Syprine Cap 250MG
Dantrium IV 20MG	Locoid Crm 0.1%	Syrex Inj 0.9%
Demser Cap 250MG	Locoid Lipocrem 0.1%	Tenormin Inj 0.5MG/ML
Dermagraft Sheet	Lymphazurin Inj 10MG/ML	Testopel Pellets 75MG
Digoxin Soln 0.05MG/1ML	Matulane Cap 50MG	Tetanus To Inj 10LF/0.5ML
Diprivan IV Emul 10MG/1ML	Maxipime Inj 1GM	Trasylol Inj 10,000kiu/ML
Diuril Sodium IV 0.5GM	Maxipime Inj 2GM	Tricitrasol Cnt 46.7%
Dopram IV Soln 20MG/1ML	MD-Gastroview 66%-10%	Tridesilon Cre 0.05%
Duramorph Inj 0.5MG/1ML	Mephyton Tab 5MG	Tridesilon Oin 0.05%
Duramorph Inj 1MG/1ML	Methylin Chew Tab 10MG	Trisenox IV Soln 1MG/1ML
Duramorph PF Inj 1MG/ML	Methylin Chew Tab 2.5MG	Tuinal Cap 50MG
Dynex Tab	Methylin Chew Tab 5MG	Uretron D/S Tab
Edecrin Sodium Inj 50MG	Methylin Soln 10MG/5ML	Utira-C Tab

Table 7. (Continued)

Nonrepackaged brand name drugs		
Name and strength of drug	**Name and strength of drug**	**Name and strength of drug**
Edecrin Tab 25MG	Methylin Soln 5MG/5ML	Virazole Sus 6GM
Elliotts B Inj	Minocin Cap 50MG	Vitrasert Imp 4.5MG
Ergotrate Tab 0.2MG	Minocin Cap 100MG	Westhroid Tab 130MG
Erythrocin Lac Inj 500MG	Muri-Lube Oil	Westhroid Tab 32.5MG
EtheDent Chew Tab 0.25MG	Mustargen IV Pwd for Soln	Westhroid Tab 65MG
EtheDent Chew Tab 0.5MG	Nascobal Gel 500mcg/0.1ML	
EtheDent Chew Tab 1MG	Nembutal Sod Inj 50MG/ML	
Fareston Tab 60MG	Nicomide Tab	
FazaClo Dis Tab 100MG	Nitropress Inj 50MG	
FazaClo Dis Tab 25MG	Norvir Cap 100MG	
Formalyde-10 Spr 10%	Norvir Sol 80MG/ML	
Fosrenol Chew Tab 500MG	Novahistine DH 7.25-2-5/5	
Geref Inj 50mcg	NovaPlus Diprivan IV 10/1	
H.P. Acthar Gel 80U/1ML	Nydrazid Inj 100MG/ML	

Source: GAO analysis of Red Book data.

Note: Following the extraordinary price increase, some drugs may have become discontinued or transferred from one manufacturer to another. In some cases, an extraordinary price increase for a drug may not be attributed to the manufacturer that currently owns the drug.

APPENDIX III. CHARACTERISTICS OF CASE STUDY DRUGS

To gain an understanding of the market dynamics leading to extraordinary price increases for brand-name drugs, we developed case studies of six brand-name drugs identified from our analysis of Red Book data. Selection for inclusion as a case study was based on several factors including price, the level of the percentage increase, whether the drug had more than one extraordinary price increase between 2000 and 2008, availability of the drug from multiple sources, and the permanence of the price increase. See table 8 for characteristics of the drugs selected for the case studies.

Table 8. Summary of Characteristics of the Six Case Study Drugs

Drug characteristics	Drug A	Drug B	Drug C	Drug D	Drug E	Drug F
Year of FDA approval	1987	1952	1969	1960	1985	1991
Year of unit price increase	2007	2001 and 2007	2004 and 2005	2004	2008	2001
Percent unit price increase[a]	1,100	1,800 and 1,300	900 and 700	100	100	1,400
Patent status at time of price increase	No patent	No patent	No patent	No patent	Under patent[b]	Under patent
Market exclusivity status at time of price increase[c]	None	None	None	None	None	None
Repackaged drug	No	No	No	No	No	Yes[d]
Year of drug acquisition[e]	2007	2001	1998	2000	N/A[f]	N/A[g]
Generic equivalent available on the market at time of price increase[h]	Yes	No	No	No	No[i]	No
Drug available through patient assistance program[j]	No	Yes	Yes	No	No	Yes[k]
Drug is considered low volume or high volume[l]	Low volume	Low volume	Low volume	Low volume	Low volume	High volume[m]

Source: GAO analysis of Red Book and interviews with drug company representatives.

Note: Changes in unit prices are calculated using average wholesale price (AWP) in Thomson Reuters' Red Book. An extraordinary price increase is a unit price increase equal to 100 percent or more at a single point in time from 2000 to 2008. Patent status is reported as of the date the extraordinary price increase occurred.

[a] Percent increase is rounded to the nearest hundred percent.

[b] This drug had a method-of-use patent.

[c] The Federal Food, Drug, and Cosmetics Act authorizes various periods of market exclusivity for new drug products. Generally, market exclusivities prevent the

Food and Drug Administration (FDA) from approving any application for a competing drug compound for a stated period of time.

[d] This drug was sold by a repackager. The price of the drug was set by the repackager and not the manufacturer.

[e] Indicates the year that the rights to the drug were acquired from the previous manufacturer. [f]This company owns the original rights to the drug.

[g] This drug was sold by a repackager.

[h] This information was obtained from the companies and publicly available information from the FDA.

[I] This drug's active ingredient is available as a generic in other dosage forms.

[j] Patient assistance programs are typically established to offer a company's drug products at low or no cost to low-income, underinsured, or uninsured individuals.

[k] This drug was sold by a repackager. At the time of its extraordinary price increase, the drug was available through the manufacturer's patient assistance program.

[l] Drug companies were asked to identify their drug as either low volume or high volume, depending on the amount manufactured annually.

[m] The manufacturer of the drug said that this drug was a high-volume product at the time of its extraordinary price increase. The repackager told us it sold a small amount of the drug at the time of its extraordinary price increase.

End Notes

[1] In this report, drug prices are measured by the AWP, a drug pricing benchmark that is commonly used in the pharmaceutical industry. AWP is in most cases the manufacturer's suggested list price and does not necessarily reflect the actual price charged by a wholesaler.

[2] Red Book is a drug pricing compendium with information about prices and other characteristics of drug products, published by Thomson Reuters.

[3] A unit price is the (1) price per gram; (2) price per milliliter; or (3) price for each piece, such as for products sold in tablets. The unit price and other characteristics of the brand-name drugs cited in this report were those recorded in the Red Book as of December 31, 2008.

[4] The name of a drug and its manufacturer, the strength of the drug, and the package size or number of units (such as tablets) in the package are represented by a 11-digit national drug code (NDC-11).

[5] Prescription drugs may be repackaged from bulk drug purchases into smaller packages and identified by the repackaging company's unique NDC. Repackaged drugs are typically sold to health care providers, who then resell them to patients.

[6] Drugs that possess a similar chemical structure and similar therapeutic effects are grouped into therapeutic classes. Most drugs within a therapeutic class produce similar benefits, side effects, adverse reactions, and interactions with other drugs and substances.

[7] For this report, companies that manufacture and/or sell brand-name drugs are referred to as drug companies.

[8] While prescription drug spending and prices continue to rise, the rate of growth in spending and prices for prescription drugs declined in 2007. In 2000, national spending for retail prescription drugs was $120.6 billion, compared to $227.5 billion in 2007—an average increase of 10 percent a year. In 2007, retail prescription drug spending grew 4.9 percent,

and prescription drug prices increased 1.4 percent. M. Hartman, A. Martin, P. McDonnell, A. Catlin, and the National Health Expenditure Accounts Team, "National Health Spending in 2007: Slower Drug Spending Contributes to Lowest Rate of Overall Growth Since 1998," *Health Affairs*, vol. 28, no. 1 (2009). However, there is preliminary indication of higher drug price increases from 2008 to 2009.

[9] To obtain FDA approval for a drug, a drug company must conduct clinical studies showing that the drug is safe and effective for its intended use, or indication.

[10] While a brand-name drug is patented, therapeutically similar brand-name drugs not containing the same active chemical ingredient, also known as "me-too" drugs, may be developed and marketed by a drug company. Also, the FDA may not approve generic therapeutic equivalents to a brand-name drug prior to the expiration of the drug's patent unless the applicant certifies that the patent is invalid or that the generic drug does not infringe the patent.

[11] Drugs obtained directly from health care providers may eliminate travel to a pharmacy to obtain a prescribed drug. In addition, the availability of repackaged drugs from the health care provider may reduce medication errors caused by poor handwriting—such as administering the wrong medication or an incorrect dosing.

[12] *See* 35 U.S.C. §§ 111, 154.

[13] Patents may be granted for several properties of a drug. For example, a drug company may obtain a patent on the active ingredient used in the drug. Companies may also obtain patents on the use of a drug, and a drug's formula and composition. Although a patent may be granted for a drug product long before its approval for marketing by the FDA, a company may obtain a patent term extension in certain circumstances.

[14] 21 U.S.C. § 355(c)(3)(D)(ii).

[15] 21 U.S.C. § 355(c)(3)(D)(iii).

[16] 21 U.S.C. § 355(j)(2)(D)(iv). Exclusivity pertains to the first applicant of an abbreviated new drug application based on a previously approved brand-name drug.

[17] 21 U.S.C. § 355a.

[18] 21 U.S.C. § 360cc. An orphan drug is a drug that treats a rare disease or condition which is generally defined as affecting fewer than 200,000 people in the United States.

[19] The FDA is responsible for designating drugs as orphan drugs.

[20] Underinsured patients typically face limited covered benefits and high out-of-pocket costs such as deductibles, coinsurance, or copayments.

[21] *See* 15 U.S.C. §§ 18, 1. In addition, states investigate and litigate potential violations of state as well as federal antitrust law. *See* 15 U.S.C. § 15c.

[22] 15 U.S.C. § 18a. Companies involved in transactions that do not meet certain criteria are not required to notify the FTC and DOJ. The FTC and DOJ may seek an injunction to halt the acquisition or require that companies divest certain drugs if they determine that the merger is likely to be anticompetitive.

[23] *See* 15 U.S.C. § 45 (prohibiting unfair methods of competition).

[24] *See* 21 C.F.R. part 211 (2009).

[25] About 90 percent of the extraordinary price increases—380 brand-name drug products—remained at the increased price for more than 90 days after experiencing the price increase, and more than four-fifths remained at the increased price for 180 days or more.

[26] We compared the price of the drug immediately after the extraordinary price increase to the last recorded price of the drug as of December 31, 2008. For 361 drugs that had extraordinary price increases, the final price recorded for these drugs was the same price or higher than the price immediately after the extraordinary price increase.

[27] The NDC-9 code represents the name of the drug and its manufacturer, and strength of the drug. The price increases for brand-name drug products that had an extraordinary price increase were reported using unit price data recorded at the NDC-9 level.

[28] These three therapeutic classes represented 40 percent of all brand-name drugs recorded in Red Book.

[29] The unit price for brand-name drug products that had an extraordinary price increase were reported using unit price data at the NDC-9 level. We report the unit price of a drug prior to the extraordinary price increase. A unit price is denoted by Thompson Reuters in Red Book as (1) price per gram; (2) price per milliliter; and (3) price for each piece, such as products sold by the item, such as tablets or capsules.

[30] Of the brand-name drug products priced less than $25 per unit prior to the extraordinary price increase, 40 percent were priced less than a dollar, 54 percent between $1 and $9.99, and 6 percent between $10 and $24.99. After the extraordinary price increase, 18 percent of these drugs were priced less than a dollar, 63 percent between $1 and $9.99, and 19 percent between $10 and $24.99.

[31] The median price after the increase is calculated using the price recorded in Red Book as of December 31, 2008, because the price of these drugs may have increased or decreased following the extraordinary price increase.

[32] The calculation of treatment cost is based on two courses of treatment lasting up to 28 days. In some cases, patients on this drug may receive only one course of treatment. The out-of-pocket cost for a patient varies depending on insurance coverage.

[33] The price increases for drugs that had an extraordinary price increase are reported using unit price data recorded at the NDC-9 level. Less than half of all brand-name drug products recorded in Red Book were repackaged drugs.

[34] To determine whether an extraordinary price increase was initiated by a drug's manufacturer or by the repackager of the drug, we matched all repackaged drugs that had an extraordinary price increase to the nonrepackaged equivalent drug brand sold by the manufacturer. To account for increases initiated by manufacturers of nonrepackaged drugs that had an increase of less than 100 percent and therefore were not captured from Red Book, we counted only repackaged drugs that had an increase of at least 200 percent for this analysis.

[35] These four repackaging companies accounted for about three quarters of all repackaged drugs that had an extraordinary price increase.

[36] As discussed earlier, the price of a course of treatment depends on the nature of the condition treated, how long the condition should be treated, and the number of units of a drug used to treat the condition.

[37] The median price after the increase is calculated using the price recorded in Red Book as of December 31, 2008, because the price of these drugs may have increased or decreased following the extraordinary price increase.

[38] For this report, we use the term therapeutically equivalent drugs to include both generic versions of a brand-name drug and other brand-name drugs used to treat the same condition. Generally, according to the FDA a therapeutically equivalent drug refers only to the generic version of a brand-name drug.

[39] Drug companies may also receive a patent for minor alterations to the formulation of a drug such as reversing only the structure of the chemical used in the active ingredient.

[40] See Apps. I and III for more details on the case study drugs.

[41] A drug's patent(s) may be acquired through grant, sale, or other type of transfer.

[42] Two companies in our case studies have acquired another drug company and its drug products. Also, some of the companies in our case studies have acquired the rights to drugs manufactured by other companies.

[43] According to the company, the previous owner sold the rights to the drug because of difficulty manufacturing the drug and its financial losses from low sales of the drug.

[44] These changes included upgrades to manufacturing equipment used to detect and reduce impurities and revalidation of the entire manufacturing process.

[45] Drug manufacturers that wish to have their drugs available for Medicaid enrollees are required to enter into rebate agreements with the federal government on behalf of states. These rebate agreements are intended to ensure that Medicaid pays the lowest price that the manufacturer offers for the drug. Rebates are computed and paid by the drug manufacturer each quarter based on drug utilization data supplied by Medicaid.

[46] The basic Medicaid rebate is 15.1 percent of a drug's average manufacturer price (AMP) per unit, or the difference between AMP and a drug's best price, whichever is greater. If a brand-name drug's AMP rises faster than inflation, as measured by the consumer price index, an additional unit rebate may be calculated. See U.S.C. § 1396r-8(c). The two companies indicated that due to the application of additional unit rebates caused by increases in their drug prices, their Medicaid rebates actually exceeded their drugs' AMPs.

[47] Unless otherwise noted, in this report "brand-name drugs" refers to brand-name prescription drugs.

[48] In this report, drug prices are measured by AWP. AWP is in most cases the manufacturer's suggested price and does not necessarily reflect the actual price charged by a wholesaler. AWP is a drug pricing benchmark that is commonly used in the pharmaceutical industry.

[49] Red Book is a proprietary database containing drug pricing and other drug-related information published by Thomson Reuters. Drug manufacturers and companies report the price of their drug—in AWP or other pricing benchmarks—to Thomson Reuters for publication in the Red Book. In some cases, Red Book calculates AWP values using other pricing benchmarks.

[50] A unit price is the (1) price per gram; (2) price per milliliter; or (3) price for each piece, such as for products sold in tablets. The unit price and other characteristics of the brand-name drugs cited in this report were those recorded in Red Book as of December 31, 2008.

[51] Drug prices are identified and reported in Red Book by an 11-digit number called the NDC-11 code. The NDC-11 code represents the name of the drug and its manufacturer, the strength of the drug, and the package size—or number of units (such as tablets) in the package.

[52] As a result, for these brand-name drugs we do not capture this variation in extraordinary price increase by package size.

[53] Prescription drugs may be repackaged from bulk drug purchases into individual dose packages and identified by the repackaging company's unique NDC. Repackaged drugs may be sold to health care providers, who then dispense them to their patients.

[54] To determine whether an extraordinary price increase was initiated by a drug's manufacturer or by the repackager of the drug, we matched all repackaged drugs that had an extraordinary price increase to the nonrepackaged equivalent drug brand sold by the manufacturer. Whenever a match between the repackaged and nonrepackaged drug was not found, we concluded that the repackaged drug had an extraordinary price increase without a corresponding increase by the drug's manufacturer for the identical nonrepackaged drug. To account for increases initiated by manufacturers of nonrepackaged drugs that had an increase of less than 100 percent and therefore were not captured from Red Book, we counted only repackaged drugs that had an increase of at least 200 percent for this analysis.

[55] We deleted records from our data files in a few cases where a drug company provided evidence showing that an extraordinary price increase had not occurred. In one case, data entry errors recording an incorrect package size was the reason for an extraordinary price increase. We also deleted one record that showed an extraordinary price increase after December 31, 2008.

[56] Red Book is a database containing drug pricing and other drug-related information published by Thomson Reuters.

[57] The NDC-9 code represents the name of the drug and its manufacturer, and strength of the drug.

In: Prescription Drug Pricing
Editors: J. R. Dickson, A. M. Woebler
ISBN: 978-1-61324-639-9

Chapter 3

OVERVIEW OF APPROACHES TO CONTROL PRESCRIPTION DRUG SPENDING IN FEDERAL PROGRAMS

John E. Dicken

WHY GAO DID THIS STUDY

Millions of individuals receive prescription drugs through federal programs. The increasing cost of prescription drugs has put pressure to control drug spending on federal programs such as the Federal Employees Health Benefits Program (FEHBP), Medicare Part D, the Department of Veterans Affairs (VA), the Department of Defense (DOD), and Medicaid. Prescription drug spending within the FEHBP in particular, which provides health and drug coverage to about 8 million federal employees, retirees, and their dependents, has been a significant contributor to FEHBP cost and premium growth. The Office of Personnel Management (OPM), which administers the FEHBP, predicted that prescription drugs would continue to be a primary driver of program costs in 2009.

GAO was asked to describe approaches used by the FEHBP to control prescription drug spending and summarize approaches used by other federal programs. This testimony is based on prior GAO work, including *Prescription Drugs: Oversight of Drug Pricing in Federal Programs* (GAO-07-481T) and *Prescription Drugs: An Overview of Approaches to Negotiate Drug Prices Used by Other Countries and U.S. Private Payers and Federal Programs*

(GAO-07-358T) and selected updates from relevant literature on drug spending controls prepared by other congressional and federal agencies.

WHAT GAO FOUND

FEHBP uses competition among health plans to control prescription drug spending, giving plans an incentive to rein in costs and leverage their market share to obtain favorable drug prices. Most FEHBP plans contract with pharmacy benefit managers (PBMs) to help administer the prescription drug benefit. In a 2003 report, GAO found that the PBMs reduced drug spending by: negotiating rebates with drug manufacturers and passing some of the savings to the plans; obtaining drug price discounts from retail pharmacies and dispensing drugs at lower costs through mail-order pharmacies operated by the PBMs; and using other techniques that reduce utilization of certain drugs or substitute other, less costly drugs. While OPM does not negotiate drug prices or discounts for FEHBP, it attempts to limit spending through annual premium and benefit negotiations with plans, including the encouragement of spending controls such as generic substitution.

Other federal programs use a range of approaches to control prescription drug spending.

- Medicare—the federal health insurance program for the elderly and disabled—offers an outpatient prescription drug benefit known as Medicare Part D that uses competition between plan sponsors and their PBMs to limit drug spending, in part through the ability to negotiate prices and price concessions with drug manufacturers and pharmacies. Plans are required to report these negotiated price concessions to the Centers for Medicare & Medicaid Services (CMS), to help CMS determine the extent to which they are passed on to beneficiaries.
- VA and DOD pharmacy benefit programs for veterans, active duty military personnel, and others may use statutorily mandated discounts as well as negotiations with drug suppliers to limit drug spending. VA and DOD have access to a number of prices to consider when purchasing drugs—including the Federal Supply Schedule prices that VA negotiates with drug manufacturers—paying the lowest of all available prices.

- The Medicaid program for low-income adults and children is subject to aggregate payment limits and drug payment guidelines set by CMS. Medicaid does not negotiate drug prices with manufacturers, but reimburses retail pharmacies for drugs dispensed to beneficiaries at set prices. An important element of controlling Medicaid drug spending is the Medicaid drug rebate program, under which drug manufacturers are required by law to provide rebates for certain drugs covered by Medicaid. Under the rebate program, states take advantage of prices manufacturers receive for drugs in the commercial market that reflect discounts and rebates negotiated by private payers.

In addition, Part D, VA and DOD, and Medicaid use techniques similar to FEHBP to limit drug spending, such as generic substitution, prior authorization, utilization review programs, or cost-sharing requirements.

Mr. Chairman and Members of the Subcommittee:

I am pleased to be here as you examine approaches to control the rising spending for prescription drugs within the Federal Employees Health Benefits Program (FEHBP). As you know, the FEHBP provides health coverage, including prescription drug coverage, to about 8 million federal employees, retirees, and their dependents. As with other public and private employer-sponsored health plans, prescription drug spending has been a significant contributor to FEHBP cost and premium growth. Projected increases in the costs of prescription drugs alone would have accounted for about a 3 to 5 percent annual increase in FEHBP premiums from 2002 through 2007. The Office of Personnel Management (OPM), the federal agency that administers the FEHBP, predicted that prescription drugs would continue to be a primary driver of program costs in 2009.[1]

Because of the importance of controlling prescription drug spending by the federal government, you asked us to describe prescription drug spending control approaches used by the FEHBP and summarize the approaches used by other federal programs. Accordingly, my testimony today will describe the approach used by FEHBP to control prescription drug spending and summarize approaches used under Medicare, the Department of Veterans Affairs (VA), the Department of Defense (DOD), and Medicaid. My remarks are based on prior work performed from 2003 to 2009 on federal programs that purchase or cover prescription drugs, with selected updates from relevant literature on drug spending controls prepared by other congressional and federal agencies.[2] We used various methodologies to complete our work; please see the individual products for the details. Our work was performed in accordance with generally accepted government auditing standards. Those standards require that we plan and perform the audit to obtain sufficient, appropriate evidence to provide a reasonable basis for our findings and conclusions based on our audit objectives. We believe that the evidence obtained provides a reasonable basis for our findings and conclusions based on our audit objectives.

BACKGROUND

The FEHBP is the largest employer-sponsored health insurance program in the country. Through it, about 8 million federal employees, retirees, and their dependents received health coverage—including for prescription drugs—in 2008. Coverage is provided under competing plans offered by multiple private health insurers under contract with OPM, which administers the program, subject to applicable requirements. In 2009, 269 health plan options were offered by participating insurers, 10 of which were offered nationally while the remaining health plan options were offered in certain geographic regions. According to OPM, plans must cover all medically necessary prescription drugs approved by the Food and Drug Administration (FDA), but plans may maintain formularies that encourage the use of certain drugs over others.[3] Enrollees may obtain prescriptions from retail pharmacies that contract with the plans or from mail-order pharmacies offered by the plans. In 2005, FEHBP prescription drug spending was an estimated $8.3 billion.

Medicare—the federal health insurance program that serves about 45 million elderly and disabled individuals—offers an outpatient prescription drug benefit known as Medicare Part D. This benefit was established by the Medicare Prescription Drug, Improvement, and Modernization Act of 2003 (MMA) beginning January 1, 2006.[4] As of February 2009, Part D provided federally subsidized prescription drug coverage for nearly 27 million beneficiaries. The Centers for Medicare & Medicaid Services (CMS), part of the Department of Health and Human Services (HHS), manages and oversees Part D. Medicare beneficiaries may choose a Part D plan from multiple competing plans offered nationally or in certain geographic areas by private sponsors, largely commercial insurers, under contract with CMS. Part D plan sponsors offer drug coverage either through stand-alone prescription drug plans for beneficiaries in traditional fee-for-service Medicare or through

Medicare managed care plans, known as Medicare Advantage. In 2009, there were over 3,700 prescription drug plans offered. Under Medicare Part D, plans can design their own formularies, but each formulary must include drugs within each therapeutic category and class of covered Part D drugs. Enrollees may obtain prescriptions from retail pharmacies that contract with the plans or from mail-order pharmacies offered by the plans. Medicare Part D spending is estimated to be about $51 billion in 2009.

The VA pharmacy benefit is provided to eligible veterans and certain others. As of 2006, about 8 million veterans were enrolled in the VA system.[5] In general, medications must be prescribed by a VA provider, filled at a VA pharmacy, and listed on the VA national drug formulary, which comprises 570 categories of drugs. In addition to the VA national formulary, VA facilities can establish local formularies to cover additional drugs. VA may provide nonformulary drugs in cases of medical necessity. In 2006, VA spent an estimated $3.4 billion on prescription drugs.

The DOD pharmacy benefit is provided to TRICARE beneficiaries, including active duty personnel, certain reservists, retired uniformed service members, and dependents.[6] As of 2009, there were about 9.4 million eligible TRICARE beneficiaries. In addition to maintaining a formulary, DOD provides options for obtaining nonformulary drugs. Beneficiaries can obtain prescription drugs through a network of retail pharmacies, nonnetwork retail pharmacies, DOD military treatment facilities, and DOD's TRICARE Mail-Order Pharmacy. In 2006, DOD spent $6.2 billion on prescription drugs.

Medicaid, a joint federal-state program, finances medical services for certain low-income adults and children.[7] In fiscal year 2008, approximately 63 million beneficiaries were enrolled in Medicaid.[8] While some benefits are federally required, outpatient prescription drug coverage is an optional benefit that all states have elected to offer. Drug coverage depends on the manufacturer's participation in the federal Medicaid drug rebate program, through which manufacturers pay rebates to state Medicaid programs for covered drugs used by Medicaid beneficiaries. Retail pharmacies distribute drugs to Medicaid beneficiaries and then receive reimbursements from states for the acquisition cost of the drug and a dispensing fee. Medicaid outpatient drug spending has decreased since 2006 because Medicare Part D replaced Medicaid as the primary source of drug coverage for low-income beneficiaries with coverage under both programs—referred to as dual eligible beneficiaries.[9] In fiscal year 2008, Medicaid outpatient drug spending was $9.3 billion—including $5.5 billion as the federal share—which was calculated after adjusting for manufacturer rebates to states under the Medicaid drug rebate program.

FEHBP Uses Competition between Health Plans to Control Prescription Drug Costs

FEHBP uses competition among health plans as the primary measure to control prescription drug spending and other program costs. Under an annual "open season," enrollees may remain enrolled in the same plan or select another competing plan based on benefits, services, premiums, and other such factors. Thus, plans have the incentive to try to retain or increase their market share by providing the benefits sought by enrollees along with competitive premiums. In turn, the larger a plan's market share, the more leverage it has for obtaining favorable drug prices on behalf of its enrollees and controlling prescription drug spending.

Similar to most private employer-sponsored or individually purchased health plans, most FEHBP plans contract with pharmacy benefit managers (PBMs) to help them administer the prescription drug benefit and control drug spending. In a 2003 report reviewing the use of PBMs by three plans representing about 55 percent of total FEHBP enrollment, we found that the PBMs used three key approaches to achieve savings for the health plans:

- negotiating rebates with drug manufacturers and passing some of the savings to the plans;
- obtaining drug price discounts from retail pharmacies and dispensing drugs at lower costs through mail-order pharmacies operated by the PBMs; and
- using other intervention techniques that reduce utilization of certain drugs or substitute other, less costly drugs.[10] For example, under generic substitution PBMs substituted less expensive, chemically equivalent generic drugs for brand-name drugs; under therapeutic interchange PBMs encouraged the substitution of less expensive formulary brand-name drugs for more expensive nonformulary drugs within the same drug class; under prior authorization PBMs required enrollees to receive approval from the plan or PBM before dispensing certain drugs that are high cost or meet other criteria; and under drug utilization review PBMs examined prescriptions at the time of

purchase or retrospectively to assess safety considerations and compliance with clinical guidelines, including appropriate quantity and dosage.

The PBMs were compensated by retaining some of the negotiated savings. The PBMs also collected fees from the plans for administrative and clinical services, kept a portion of the payments from FEHBP plans for mail-order drugs in excess of the prices they paid manufacturers to acquire the drugs, and in some cases retained a share of the rebates that PBMs negotiated with drug manufacturers.[11]

While OPM does not play a role in negotiating prescription drug prices or discounts, it does attempt to limit prescription drug spending through its leverage with participating health plans in annual premium and benefit negotiations. Each year, OPM negotiates benefit and rate proposals with participating plans and announces key policy goals for the program, including those relating to spending control. For example, in preparation for benefit and rate negotiations for the 2007 plan year, OPM encouraged proposals from plans to continue to explore the appropriate substitution for higher cost drugs with lower cost therapeutic alternatives, such as generic drugs, and the use of tiered formularies or prescription drug lists. OPM also sought proposals from plans to pursue the advantages of specialty pharmacy programs aimed at reducing the high costs of infused and intravenously administered drugs.[12] In preparation for 2010 benefit and rate negotiations, OPM reiterated its desire for proposals from plans to substitute lower cost for higher cost therapeutically equivalent drugs, adding emphasis to using evidence-based health outcome measures.[13]

OTHER FEDERAL PROGRAMS USE A RANGE OF APPROACHES TO CONTROL PRESCRIPTION DRUG SPENDING

Medicare Part D uses a competitive model similar to FEHBP, while other federal programs use other methods, such as statutorily mandated prices or direct negotiations with drug suppliers.

Medicare Part D Uses Competing Prescription Drug Plans

Medicare Part D follows a model similar to the FEHBP by relying on competing prescription drug plans to control prescription drug spending. As with the FEHBP, during an annual open season Part D enrollees may remain enrolled in the same plan or select from among other competing plans based on benefit design, premiums, and other plan features. To attract enrollees, plans have the incentive to offer benefits that will meet beneficiaries' prescription drug needs at competitive premiums. The larger a plan's market share, the more leverage it has for obtaining favorable drug prices on behalf of its enrollees and controlling prescription drug spending. As a result, Part D plans vary in their monthly premiums, the annual deductibles, and cost sharing for drugs. Plans also differ in the drugs they cover on their formulary and the pharmacies they use.

Part D uses competing sponsors to generate prescription drug savings for beneficiaries, in part through their ability to negotiate prices with drug manufacturers and pharmacies. To generate these savings, sponsors often contract with PBMs to negotiate rebates with drug manufacturers, discounts with retail pharmacies, and other price concessions on behalf of the sponsor. MMA specifically states that the Secretary of HHS may not interfere with negotiations between sponsors and drug manufacturers and pharmacies.[14] Even though CMS is not involved in price negotiations, it attempts to determine whether beneficiaries are receiving the benefit of negotiated drug prices and price concessions when it calculates the final plan payments. Sponsors must report the price concession amounts to CMS and pass price concessions onto beneficiaries and the program through lower cost sharing, lower drug prices, or lower premiums. Similar to OPM, CMS also negotiates plan design with participating plans and announces key policy goals for the program, including those relating to spending control. For example, in preparation for 2010 benefit and rate negotiations, CMS noted that one of its goals is to establish a more transparent process so that beneficiaries will be able to better predict their out-of-pocket costs.

Part D sponsors or their PBMs also use other methods to help contain drug spending similar to FEHBP plans. For example, most plans assign covered drugs to distinct tiers, each of which carries a different level of cost sharing. A plan may establish separate tiers for generic drugs and brand-name drugs—with the generic drug tier requiring a lower level of cost sharing than the brand-name drug tier. Plans may also require utilization management for certain drugs on their formulary. Common utilization management practices include requiring physicians to obtain authorization from the plan prior to prescribing a drug; step therapy, which requires beneficiaries to first try a less costly drug to treat their condition; and imposing quantity limits for dispensed drugs. Additionally, all Part D plans must meet requirements with respect to the extent of their pharmacy networks[15] and the categories of drugs they must cover.[16] Plan formularies generally must cover at least two Part D drugs in each therapeutic category and class, except when there is only one drug in the category or class or when CMS has allowed the plan to cover only one drug.[17] CMS has also designated six categories of drugs of clinical concern for which plans must cover all or substantially all of the drugs.[18]

VA and DOD Use Statutorily Mandated Prices and Negotiate Directly with Drug Suppliers

While FEHBP and Medicare Part D use competition between health plans to control prescription drug spending, VA and DOD rely on statutorily mandated prices and discounts and further negotiations with drug suppliers to obtain lower prices for drugs covered on their formularies.

VA and DOD have access to a number of prices to consider when purchasing drugs, paying the lowest available.

- *Federal Supply Schedule (FSS) prices.* VA's National Acquisition Center negotiates FSS prices with drug manufacturers, and these prices are available to all direct federal purchasers.[19] FSS prices are intended to be no more than the prices manufacturers charge their most-favored nonfederal customers under comparable terms and conditions. Under federal law, drug manufacturers must list their brand-name drugs on the FSS to receive reimbursement for drugs covered by Medicaid.[20] All FSS prices include a fee of 0.5 percent of the price to fund VA's National Acquisition Center.
- *Federal ceiling prices.* Federal ceiling prices, also called Big Four prices, are available to VA, DOD, thc Public Health Service, and the U.S. Coast Guard. These prices are mandated by law to be 24 percent lower than nonfederal average manufacturer prices.[21]
- *Blanket purchase agreements and other national contracts.* Blanket purchase agreements and other national contracts with drug manufacturers allow VA and DOD—either separately or jointly—to negotiate prices below FSS prices. The lower prices may depend on

the volume of specific drugs being purchased by particular facilities, such as VA or military hospitals, or on being assigned preferred status on VA's and DOD's respective national formularies.

In a few cases, individual VA and DOD medical centers have obtained lower prices through local agreements with suppliers than they could have through the national contracts, FSS prices, or federal ceiling prices.

In addition, VA's and DOD's use of formularies, pharmacies, and prime vendors can further affect drug prices and help control drug spending. Both VA and DOD use their own national, standard formulary to obtain more competitive prices from manufacturers that have their drugs listed on the formulary. VA and DOD formularies also encourage the substitution of lower cost drugs determined to be as or more effective than higher cost drugs. VA and DOD use prime vendors, which are preferred drug distributors, to purchase drugs from manufacturers and deliver the drugs to VA or DOD facilities. VA and DOD receive discounts from their prime vendors that also reduce the prices that they pay for drugs. For DOD, the discounts vary among prime vendors and the areas they serve. As of June 2004, VA's prime vendor discount was 5 percent, while DOD's discounts averaged about 2.9 percent within the United States. Additionally, similar to FEHBP and Medicare Part D, DOD uses utilization management methods to limit drug spending including prior authorization, dispensing limitations, and higher cost sharing for nonformulary drugs and drugs dispensed at retail pharmacies.

Medicaid Uses Aggregate Payment Limits, Drug Pricing Guidelines, and Required Rebates

Unlike VA and DOD, Medicaid programs do not negotiate drug prices with manufacturers to control prescription drug spending, but reimburse retail pharmacies for drugs dispensed to beneficiaries at set prices. CMS sets aggregate payment limits—known as the federal upper limit (FUL)—for certain outpatient multiple-source prescription drugs.[22] CMS also provides guidelines regarding drug payment. States are to pay pharmacies the lower of the state's estimate of the drug's acquisition cost to the pharmacy, plus a dispensing fee, or the pharmacy's usual and customary charge to the general public; for certain drugs the FUL or the state maximum allowable costs may apply if lower.[23]

In addition to these retail pharmacy reimbursements, Medicaid programs also control prescription drug spending through the Medicaid drug rebate program.[24] Under the drug rebate program, drug manufacturers are required to provide quarterly rebates for covered outpatient prescription drugs purchased by state Medicaid programs. Under the rebate program, states take advantage of the prices manufacturers receive for drugs in the commercial market that reflect the results of negotiations by private payers such as discounts and rebates. For brand-name drugs, the rebates are based on two price benchmarks per drug that manufacturers report to CMS: best price[25] and average manufacturer price (AMP).[26] The relationship between best price and AMP determines the unit rebate amount and thus the overall size of the rebate that states receive. The basic unit rebate amount is the greater of two values: the difference between best price and AMP or 15.1 percent of AMP. If the brand-name drug's AMP rises faster than inflation as measured by the change in the consumer price index, the manufacturer is required to provide an additional rebate to the state Medicaid program. In addition to brand-name drugs, states also receive rebates for generic drugs. For generic drugs, the basic unit rebate amount is 11 percent of the AMP. A state's rebate for a drug is the product of the unit rebate amount plus any applicable additional rebate amount and the number of units of the drug paid for by the state's Medicaid program. In addition to the rebates mandated under the drug rebate program, states can also negotiate additional rebates with manufacturers.

Like FEHBP and Medicare Part D participating plans, Medicaid programs also use other utilization management methods to control prescription drug spending including prior authorization and utilization review programs, dispensing limitations, and cost-sharing requirements.

Mr. Chairman, this concludes my prepared remarks. I would be happy to answer any questions that you or other members of the Subcommittee may have.

End Notes

[1] OPM, *News Release: OPM Announces Open Season for Health Benefits, Dental and Vision Insurance, and Flexible Spending Accounts* (Sept. 25, 2008).

[2] A list of related GAO products is included at the end of this statement. For other reports we reviewed, please see, for example, *Congressional Budget Office, Budget Options Volume 1: Health Care* (Washington, D.C.: Dec. 2008); *Congressional Budget Office, The Health Care System for Veterans: An Interim Report* (Washington, D.C.: Dec. 2007); *Congressional Research Service, Medicare Part D Prescription Drug Benefit: A Primer* (Washington, D.C.: Aug. 20, 2008); *Congressional Research Service, Prescription Drug*

Coverage Under Medicaid (Washington, D.C.: Feb. 6, 2008); *Congressional Research Service, Pharmaceutical Costs: A Comparison of Department of Veterans Affairs (VA), Medicaid, and Medicare Policies* (Washington, D.C.: Apr. 13, 2007); *Federal Trade Commission, Pharmacy Benefit Managers: Ownership of Mail-Order Pharmacies* (Washington, D.C.: Aug. 2005); and *Medicare Payment Advisory Commission, Report to the Congress: Medicare Payment Policy* (Washington, D.C.: Mar. 2009).

[3] Formularies include lists of prescription drugs, grouped by therapeutic class (groups of drugs that are similar in chemistry, method of action, and purpose of use), that health plans or insurers encourage physicians to prescribe and beneficiaries to use.

[4] Pub. L. No. 108-173, § 101, 117 Stat. 2066, 2071-2152 (codified at 42 U.S.C. §§ 1395w-101 to 1395w-152). MMA redesignated the previous part D of title XVIII of the Social Security Act as part E and inserted a new part D after part C.

[5] Of the almost 8 million veterans enrolled, about 5 million received health care services. Additionally, there were over 4 million pharmacy users in VA in 2006.

[6] DOD provides health care through TRICARE—a regionally structured program that uses contractors to maintain provider networks to complement health care provided at military treatment facilities.

[7] Medicaid consists of 56 distinct programs created within broad federal guidelines and administered by state Medicaid agencies. The 56 Medicaid programs include 1 for each of the 50 states; the District of Columbia; Puerto Rico; and the U.S. territories of American Samoa, Guam, Northern Mariana Islands, and the Virgin Islands. Within a framework established by federal statutes, regulations, and policies, each state (1) establishes its own eligibility standards; (2) determines the type, amount, duration, and scope of services; (3) sets the rate of payment for services; and (4) administers its own program.

[8] Approximately 6 million of the 63 million Medicaid beneficiaries were 65 years or older in 2008.

[9] Part D includes different levels of premium and cost-sharing assistance for dual eligible beneficiaries as well as assistance for other eligible beneficiaries who have low incomes and modest assets but do not meet the eligibility requirements for Medicaid.

[10] GAO, *Federal Employees' Health Benefits: Effects of Using Pharmacy Benefit Managers on Health Plans, Enrollees, and Pharmacies*, GAO-03-196 (Washington, D.C.: Jan. 10, 2003).

[11] In the private market, one of the key ways PBMs influence price negotiations with manufacturers is through formulary development and management. PBMs may assist health plans in developing or managing a formulary that the health plan will cover. Manufacturers pay PBMs through rebates or other payments to be included on plan formularies and to capture greater market share for their drugs.

[12] *U.S. Office of Personnel Management Insurance Services Program, Federal Employees Health Benefits Program Call Letter No. 2006-09* (Washington, D.C.: Apr. 4, 2006).

[13] *U.S. Office of Personnel Management Insurance Services Program, Federal Employees Health Benefits Program Call Letter No. 2009-08* (Washington, D.C.: Apr. 20, 2009).

[14] The Secretary may also not require a particular formulary or institute a price structure for the reimbursement of Medicare Part D drugs. Pub. L. No. 108-173, § 101, 117 Stat. 2066, 2098 (codified at 42 U.S.C. § 1395w-111(i)).

[15] All prescription drug plans must have a contracted pharmacy in their network that is within 2 miles of 90 percent of urban beneficiaries, 5 miles of 90 percent of suburban beneficiaries, and 15 miles of 70 percent of rural beneficiaries. 42 C.F.R. §423.120(a)(1)(2008).

[16] Under the MMA, prescription drug plans must cover drugs within each therapeutic category and class of Part D drugs. Pub. L. No. 108-173, § 101, 117 Stat. 2066, 2085 (codified at 42 U.S.C. § 1395w-104(b)(3)(C)).

[17] 42 C.F.R. §423.120(b)(2)(2008).

[18] Part D plan formularies must include all or substantially all drugs in the immunosuppressant, antidepressant, antipsychotic, anticonvulsant, antiretroviral, and antineoplastic drug categories.

[19] VA and DOD directly purchase drugs from manufacturers for their beneficiaries. FEHBP, Medicare Part D, and Medicaid provide reimbursement for drugs dispensed to beneficiaries.

[20] See 38 U.S.C. § 8126(a)(4).

[21] See 38 U.S.C. § 8126(a)(2). The nonfederal average manufacturer price is the weighted average price of a single form and dosage unit paid by wholesalers to a manufacturer, taking into account cash discounts or similar price reductions. Big Four prices, in general, do not apply to generic drugs.

[22] Federal regulations set specific limits for multiple-source drugs for which there are two or more therapeutically equivalent products.

[23] States may establish their own methodologies for estimating retail pharmacies' drug acquisition costs. Most states choose to estimate these costs by taking a percentage discount from the average wholesale price. The usual and customary charge for a drug is the full retail price that individuals without prescription drug coverage pay when purchasing drugs at a retail pharmacy. Some states also administer a maximum allowable cost program for selected multiple-source drugs with the maximum price at which the state will reimburse those medications.

[24] See 42 U.S.C. § 1396r-8.

[25] Best price is the lowest price available from the manufacturer to any wholesaler, retailer, provider, health maintenance organization, or nonprofit or government entity, with some exceptions. Among other things, sales made through the FSS, single-award contract prices of any federal agency, federal depot prices, and prices charged to DOD, VA, Indian Health Service, and Public Health Service are not considered in determining best price.

[26] AMP is defined by statute as the average price paid to a manufacturer for a drug by wholesalers for drugs distributed to the retail pharmacy class of trade. Under the rebate agreement manufacturers negotiate with HHS, AMP does not include prices to government purchasers based on the FSS, prices from direct sales to hospitals or health maintenance organizations, or prices to wholesalers when they relabel drugs they purchase under their own label.

In: Prescription Drug Pricing
Editors: J. R. Dickson, A. M. Woebler
ISBN: 978-1-61324-639-9

Chapter 4

OPENING STATEMENT OF U.S. SENATOR AMY KLOBUCHAR, HEARING ON "AT WHAT COST? EGREGIOUS PRICE INCREASES IN THE PHARMACEUTICAL DRUG INDUSTRY"

July 24, 2008

Thank you for attending this important hearing on rising prices of prescription drugs.

I will be introducing each panelist after opening remarks, but I'd like to thank each of them for taking the time out of their busy schedule to join us today and share their experiences and expertise.

First, I'd like to thank Danielle Foltz for her courageous effort to share her family's experience with us today. Her passionate advocacy has brought to light how decisions made in boardrooms affect families across the country.

I would also like to thank Madeline Carpenelli of the PRIME Institute, based in my home state of Minnesota, for her effort to provide context and insight into the impact of drug pricing. She has been working with Dr. Steve Schondelmeyer, who began collecting data on cases of enormous, overnight drug increases since the 1980s.

It is his work, along with Ms. Carpenelli's expertise from spending almost a decade at the Health and Human Services' Office of the Inspector General that has allowed us to examine the big picture of what these increases have done to patients with rare diseases.

And I'd like to extend special thanks to Dr. Alan Goldbloom, the CEO of Children's Hospitals and Clinics of Minnesota.

Since last July, I've worked with Children's several times in connection with the case of Abbey Taylor, the little girl who died after being seriously injured in a wading pool last summer.

This hospital is dedicated to the care of their young patients. They know how important it is for children to have access to affordable, quality health care.

That's why we're here this afternoon.

We are here because we are outraged by what some pharmaceutical companies have been doing with pricing for important medications that affect all generations. These are drugs that, because of aggressive pricing practices, have seen dramatic increases in cost. Often times, because of a limited market or other factors, the drug's price is more likely to remain at that astronomical level.

I first became aware of this issue when I received word from Children's Hospital in Minneapolis that the price for a drug called Indocin I.V. had increased substantially. It's a medication used to treat patent ductus arteriosis also called PDA, a disorder that prevents holes from healing in the hearts of premature infants.

Since its approval in the 1970s, the drug has become the most commonly-used method for treating this condition.

Two years ago, Ovation Pharmaceuticals acquired the rights to this drug from Merck. The company quickly increased the price by more than 18 times — from $100 to $1,875 — for three one-milligram units of the drug.

Even though it's an American company, the price they charge in the United States is now 44 times higher than what they sell it for in Canada, nothing can justify that kind of huge price disparity.

As it happens, there is only one other drug approved by the FDA for this heart problem —a formulation of intravenous Ibuprofen. Ovation is also the sole source of that drug in the United States and, not surprisingly, the price it charges for this medicine is nearly identical to what it charges for Indocin I.V.

A number of other Ovation products have seen similar drastic price increases. Drugs that — like Indocin - have been around for a long time and are the premier treatments for a number of diseases.

In a recent article in the medical journal *Pediatrics,* Dr. Alan H. Jobe of Cincinnati Children's Hospital described Ovation's pricing of its two drugs for the premature babies' heart condition as "quite extraordinary."

He wrote: "Words such as `unconscionable,' `unethical' and 'socially irresponsible' come to mind."

So the issue we have is that an upstart company purchases a number of drugs from another company, and even though these drugs had been on the market for years, the upstart company increases the price drastically.

But Ovation isn't the only company engaging in this disturbing trend.

Questcor Pharmaceuticals was once losing money at a rate of $1 million a month. The company's fortunes turned around after they purchased HP Acthar from Aventis. This drug was approved in the 1970s to treat multiple sclerosis, but it is now primarily the "gold-standard" for treating infantile spasms, a disorder that affects about 2000 families in the U.S.

Prior to Questcor's purchase of the drug, the wholesale price of HP Acthar was about $1600 per vial. Once in Questcor's hands the price of the drug skyrocketed to $23,000 per vial — that's a 14-fold increase!

And according to the PRIME Institute, we're hitting just the tip of the iceberg, because the problem isn't isolated to drugs that benefit small numbers of patients.

Abbott Pharmaceuticals increased the price of Norvir, a drug used to treat AIDS. The drug was often used by other companies as an ingredient in their drug therapies. In 2003, Abbott jacked up the price of Norvir ["NORE-veer"] by 400 percent.

This was done at the same time that Abbott began marketing their new product, Kaletra, another AIDS pharmaceutical drug that included Norvir and served as a replacement for the competition's drug therapy. The result forced patients and providers to turn to Abbott's Kaletra instead of the formerly cost-effective alternative that used Norvir and competitor's drugs.

Previously undisclosed documents and emails reviewed by *The Wall Street Journal* in 2007 show that Abbott's leadership actively considered ways to promote Kaletra over Norvir.

This bar graph illustrates the drastic jump in price, an egregious increase from $257 to $1285.

This chart shows just a few examples of enormous drug price increases. Mustargen to treat rare cancers, 1000 percent increase! Cosmegen to treat kidney disease, 3500 percent increase!

And the price increase for Matulane is nearly off the chart with an 8000 percent increase!

This seems to be simple price gouging to me. And it not only hurts hospitals that have to purchase these expensive drugs, but also the patients who rely on them.

An elderly woman from Park Rapids, Minnesota who suffers from cutaneous T-cell lymphoma was forced to pay over $8000 in out-of-pocket expenses for Mustargen, a drug sold by Ovation Pharmaceuticals whose single dose price increased from around $50 to nearly $550 after the company acquired the rights to the drug.

In March, I had the opportunity to meet the Benson family and their twin girls Anna and Sophia. Sophia suffered from PDA and needed Indocin I.V. for treatment. They were able to receive the drug through Children's Hospital, but with such obscene price increases, it is getting more and more difficult for providers to meet such runaway costs.

What is the solution?

In America, we have a serious problem with health care inflation and runaway costs. It's no wonder: When we have pharmaceutical companies like Ovation or Questcor increasing prices to astronomical levels because of the lack of competition in the market, their actions are able to exploit an extremely vulnerable and captive market.

And it's not like the pharmaceutical industry is withering on the vine. This chart shows that even when compared to other Fortune 500 companies, pharmaceutical company profits are much higher.

The Orphan Drug Act was passed in 1983 to provide incentives to drug companies to develop innovative drugs for rare diseases because without incentives, drug companies may never be able to recoup research and development costs in niche markets.

What we've seen, however, is that at least a handful of drug companies have used this "status" of orphan drugs to keep increasing costs—well beyond the costs of research, development, and manufacturing. These staggeringly high prices, in turn, threaten the financial stability of middle class families relying on the drugs.

Where generic drugs have helped lower the cost of many prescription drugs on the market, generic competition is also less likely to occur for orphan drugs. According to a study published in the *RAND Journal of Economics,* the market size for a drug has to be $32 million (in 2007 dollars adjusted for inflation) to ensure entry of a generic into the market.

When we're talking about drugs that have been around for decades and treat patient populations of only a few thousand, there is often just not enough of an incentive for a generic drug to enter the market.

Beyond hospitals and patients, a dramatic, unforeseeable increase in price for one of these drugs has a significant impact on the federal government. If the wholesale cost of a drug goes up, Medicaid or Medicare has to pay for the increase.

We are holding this hearing to uncover this practice, but also to look forward at what we can do to curb the dramatic increase of drug prices we've seen in the last few years.

I've asked the Federal Trade Commission to initiate an investigation into any potential anticompetitive conduct or consequence arising out of Ovation's market actions and dominance in the area of non-surgical treatments for PDA.

We need to ensure that the FTC continues to conduct these crucial investigations to guarantee competition—keeping costs low for consumers and encouraging innovation.

It's disturbing that our providers, hospitals and patients are being blindsided by these exorbitant price increases. Our federal government should be able to track these trends in pharmaceutical pricing. If we start to monitor this data, there is more of a paper trail, giving us enhanced ability to do something about these companies' practices.

When provided with the right information on drug prices, especially in smaller markets, doctors can be alerted of big price increases, potentially spurring generic alternatives to expensive drugs and giving the Centers for Medicare and Medicaid Services (CMS) the tools and information to better track pricing activity in the market.

Finally, I intend to investigate whether the FDA can fast-track approval for generic drugs that would be just as safe and effective, but much less expensive, creating competition in markets with dramatic price increases.

I understand that we have a market-based economy. It's fine for companies to make money on the products they sell. But when you're dealing with the well-being of sick patients — babies and the elderly and everyone in between — there has to be special consideration.

I look forward to hearing our witnesses' thoughts on this important issue, and I hope today marks a starting point for addressing the problems that accompany such enormous price increases. Problems that have been plaguing doctors, insurance companies, Medicare and Medicaid programs, and most importantly, the patient, for far too long.

After openings, I will introduce our panelists, and we will hear their testimony.

In: Prescription Drug Pricing
Editors: J. R. Dickson, A. M. Woebler
ISBN: 978-1-61324-639-9

Chapter 5

STATEMENT OF SENATOR CHARLES E. SCHUMER, CHAIRMAN, JOINT ECONOMIC COMMITTEE, HEARING ON "AT WHAT COST? EGREGIOUS PRICE INCREASES IN THE PHARMACEUTICAL DRUG INDUSTRY"

I'd like to thank Senator Klobuchar for holding this important hearing, and thank our witnesses for being here today.

Yesterday we talked about the Middle Class Squeeze and how American families gather around their kitchen tables and talk about how they're going to pay these skyrocketing bills for food, gasoline, college, day care, and yes – prescription drugs and health care. Today's hearing focuses on the lack of affordability of potentially lifesaving drugs that treat rare diseases.

And we're not talking about an everyday kind of un-affordability. We are talking about drugs that have gone up 100, 500, or 3,000 percent in a matter of months, weeks, or overnight. That's way more than inflation, and it far outpaces the increases families are paying for so many of their other household expenses.

Our health care system can, and usually does provide high quality care, but more and more we hear about significant problems with access and affordability hurting American patients.

While we are talking about smaller segments of our population when we discuss rare diseases, the total *number* of American families touched by them is quite high. NIH estimates that between 9 and 10 percent of the American population, or nearly 30 million men, women, and children, are affected by a rare disease. Approximately half of these people are children, and many of these rare diseases are present at birth.

Patients with rare diseases and their families suffer from more than their disease alone. They also have the frustrations of not being able to find information about their disease and the heartbreak of finding out that there is no treatment, or in the case of a witness we will hear from today, that the life-saving treatment she needs for her child is priced exorbitantly high.

When our panelist, Danielle Foltz, needed the drug Acthar (*ACT- Thar*) to treat her infant son for life- threatening epileptic spasms, she faced paying over $29,000 per vial. That's 13 times higher than the price had been just eight months before he was diagnosed. One might say that a brand new drug that just hit the market might be pricey because it had to recoup research and development expenditures, but Acthar has been on the market for *three decades*.

And the same is true for the drug Matulane (*matt-you-lane*), which treats Hodgkins Lymphoma, and cost less than $70 per dose in late 2004. Just six months later, the price had increased to $5,568! That's an *eight thousand percent* increase. And not for a groundbreaking new drug -- for a drug that was put on the market in the 1960s.

Our witnesses today are going to shine a light on practices that look uncomfortably like an abuse of the pricing power we give to drug companies. In case after case, it appears that PHARMA companies have been taking critical drugs that have been on the market for years – with the costs of their development long since paid for – and increasing prices to the very highest levels the market will bear.

Our witness from the PRIME Institute at the University of Minnesota has found over one hundred cases since 2002 where the price of single-source drugs more than doubled due to a single price increase.

Healthcare reform is on the horizon, and the appropriate pricing of drugs and all medical services should be a top priority.

We all benefit from incredible innovation of pharmaceutical companies. Their success is in treating or sometimes curing diseases both severe and mundane is an important part of American competitiveness and greatness.

But the testimonies today are disturbing and show that much greater oversight and perhaps even significant action by the Congress is needed.

Along those lines, together with Senator Klobuchar I've asked the General Accounting Office (GAO) to look into the issue of these price increases and see if they are truly justified.

I also introduced a bill and worked to develop the Senate compromise with Chairman Kennedy and Senators Clinton, Enzi and Hatch on creation of a pathway for generic versions of biologic drugs. I am pleased that the National Organization for Rare Diseases touted the passage of a pathway for follow-on biologics in their submission for the record of this hearing. That is one clear way we can help patients with rare diseases.

Creating this pathway is an important development for American consumers, and I bet that the next Administration will work with Congress to make sure that the FDA implements this priority.

Generics and market competition works. We need to build on these successes and improve our system of approval and licensing for generics. The research shows that it usually takes at least two or three generic entrants to seriously lower drug prices. It also shows that generic companies are reluctant to enter markets for rare diseases, since many of these "niche" markets aren't large enough to sustain more than one or two competitor drugs.

Of course we realize that there are legitimate reasons why drug companies may need to raise prices. Price increases can be a normal cost of doing business. But we can't let the cost of doing business serve as an all- purpose excuse for excessive pricing that put important drugs out the reach of many families.

We owe it to all of America's patients to keep a vigilant watch on this situation.

Witnesses:

Madeline Carpinelli, Institute for Pharmaceutical Research in Management and Economics at the University of Minnesota

Alan Goldbloom, CEO of Minnesota Children's Hospital

Danielle Foltz, Parent of young patient from Rhode Island

In: Prescription Drug Pricing
Editors: J. R. Dickson, A. M. Woebler
ISBN: 978-1-61324-639-9

Chapter 6

Statement of Madeline M. Carpinelli, Stephen W. Schondelmeyer, PRIME Institute, College of Pharmacy, University of Minnesota, before the Joint Economic Committee, Hearing on "Extraordinary Price Increases in the Pharmaceutical Market"

Thank you, Chairman Schumer and other members of the Joint Economic Committee for this opportunity to provide information and insights regarding pricing trends in the pharmaceutical market.

I am Madeline Carpinelli and I serve as a Research Fellow with the PRIME Institute at the University of Minnesota. This Institute focuses its research on policy issues related to pharmaceutical economics and the distribution and management of drug expenditures at all levels in the marketplace. Prior to joining the PRIME Institute, I was a senior policy analyst at the Office of Inspector General (OIG) for HHS, where I managed a team of analysts in conducting evaluations of government drug price reporting and compliance issues. During my tenure at the OIG, I played a significant role in the development of the OIG's annual Work Plan related to identification of key issues in the pharmaceutical industry such as the role of AWP, AMP and the Public Health Services' 340B Drug Program. I also interfaced with the Department of Justice and the OIG Office of Prosecutions and Investigations.

These remarks present my own findings and views based upon my experience in studying the pharmaceutical marketplace for the past nine years and upon my observations and ongoing work in collaboration with Dr. Stephen W. Schondelmeyer, the Director of the PRIME Institute.

Today, I will provide an overview and preliminary findings from research we have been conducting on *extraordinary* price increases in the pharmaceutical market. Through our tracking of drug prices over time, we have become aware that certain drug products have experienced *extraordinary* price increases that are well beyond what would normally be expected in a competitive market. We found hundreds of cases of *extraordinary* price increases for branded drug products. We also found that the incidence of such extraordinary price increases has been rising sharply in recent years, and today is much higher than it was in the 1980s and 1990s.

TRACKING DRUG PRICES AND RELATED TRENDS

Tracking changes in the benchmark prices of prescription drugs is important since it provides an explanation of the role of price changes in drug expenditures over time. AARP and the PRIME Institute have routinely tracked the price changes experienced by the brand name and generic prescription drugs most commonly used by Medicare recipients. These price change reports are updated quarterly and the reports can be found on the AARP website (www.AARP.org). These price trend reports have shown that a representative market basket of the most commonly used brand name drugs has experienced price increases from 2006 to 2007 that averaged 7.4%. For the same time period, the rate of general inflation, as measured by the Consumer Price Index for All Items, was 2.9%. In other words, brand name drug prices grew at more than two and one-half times the rate of general inflation.

Certain commonly used brand name drugs experience price increases that are substantially greater than other brand name drugs on average. For example, in 2007, Ambien (5 mg and 10 mg tablets) had an annualized price increase of 27.7% compared to the overall brand name inflation rate of 7.4%. Brand name prices that increase at a rate of two to three times the rate of general inflation have persisted for more than a decade. Each time the price trends are examined there are a handful of brand name prescription drugs that have price increases substantially greater than the overall brand name inflation rate. The impact of these prices growing faster than general inflation has been that prescription drugs have been growing as a share of national health expenditures and as a share of the gross domestic product.

While tracking the price changes of the most commonly used brand name and generic drugs, the prices of other drug products beyond the top 200 to 300 drugs have also been examined. In recent years, some of these less commonly used prescription drug products have had *extraordinary* price increases.

EXTRAORDINARY DRUG PRICE INCREASES

What do we mean by an *extraordinary* price increase? *Extraordinary* is a term that can be understood in contrast to the ordinary. Ordinarily brand name price increases have been two to three times the rate of general inflation and this rate of price increase has become routine. This rate of inflation is not necessarily acceptable, or even reflective of an economically efficient pharmaceutical market, but it has come to be expected in recent years. Even the fact that certain brand name drugs have price increases that are two to three times the average rate of inflation for most brand name drugs has come to be expected. Price increases of these certain brand name drugs may be 10% to 30% on an annual basis.

We should not minimize the impact that these brand name price increases have on public and private drug expenditures each year, or the concern that these price increases raise for patients, payers, and policymakers. Recently, however, there have been other prescription drug products that have had *extraordinary* price increases which are far beyond these already substantial price increases observed for major brand name drug products.

In order to examine, and understand, the magnitude of these *extraordinary* price increases, the PRIME Institute has been conducting a study of such price increases. For purposes of this study:

Extraordinary price increases are:

'any price increase that is equal to, or greater than, 100% at a single point in time.'

A 100% increase in price means that the price of a drug has doubled overnight. In other words, a prescription that costs $100 today would cost $200 tomorrow. Other levels of price increases may well deserve the label as *extraordinary* price increases, but a price that more than doubles all at once is certainly *extraordinary*. A price increase of this magnitude could also be labeled as a *supra competitive price* indicating that the price is achieved through some real, or perceived, monopoly position in the market.

The benchmark prices known as AWP and WAC are set, or influenced, by the drug firm. These are publicly available prices and changes in these prices will lead to changes in expenditures of public and private drug programs. Our work on this study is ongoing, but we have preliminary descriptive data on the extent of *extraordinary* price increases.

The price history of each drug product, at the NDC (national drug code) level, was examined to determine the direction and amount of price change in both of the usual benchmark prices (i.e., AWP and WAC). There was a total of 35,143 NDCs that have been introduced to the market since 1987 and this set of NDCs was used as the data set for the study. More than one-half of these drug products (18,124 NDCs) were manufactured, or at least marketed, by the firm whose name is on the label. The remaining 17,019 NDCs are drug products that are sold by firms known as repackagers. An examination of the role, practices, and pricing of these repackagers will be the subject of a later analysis.

The drug products were grouped by their patent and exclusivity status into three broad groups: (1) brand single source drugs, (2) brand off-patent drugs, and (3) generic off- patent drugs. Price changes for brand name drug products have been the initial focus of our research. Across all drug product groups, 13.5% of all NDCs have had one or more *extraordinary* price increases in the period 1988 to 2008. One in twenty (5.3%) of the brand single source NDCs and one in forty-five (2.2%) of the brand off-patent NDCs had seen an *extraordinary* price increase.

The timing of when these *extraordinary* price increases occurred was examined over the twenty year period from 1988 to 2008. While there were a few *extraordinary* price increases in the decade of the 1990s, the vast majority have been seen since the year 2000. The number of *extraordinary* price increases has been growing, and especially for brand name single source and brand name off-patent NDCs, in the past four years (See Figure 1).

A price increase of 100% or more at one point in time is remarkable in its own right, but the size of some of these *extraordinary* price increases is staggering. For the brand single source drug products there were 6 price increases of more than 1,000% with the largest being 3,436%. Another 6 brand single source NDCs had an increase between 500% and 999%. One of the brand off-patent NDCs had a price increase of 10,631% and another 10 NDCs had *extraordinary* price increases of greater than 500%.

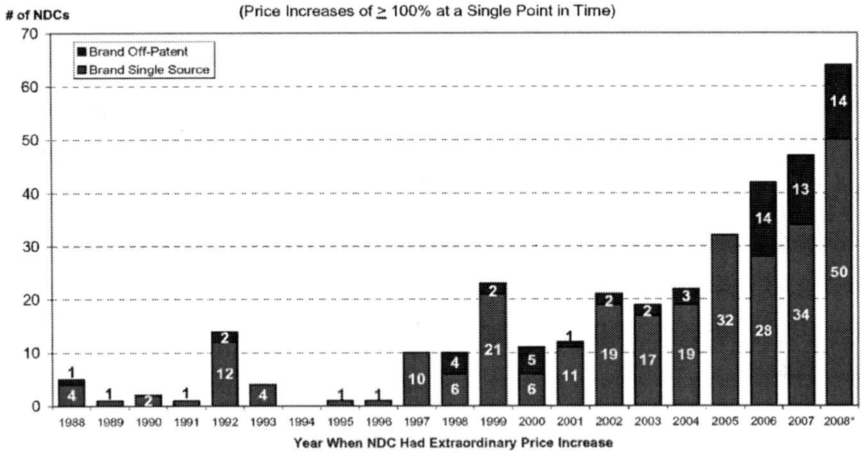

Source: Compiled by the PRIME Institute, University of Minnesota from data found in Price Chek PC (Wolters Kluwer Health, Inc., Indianapolis, IN, June 4 2008). Extraordinary price increase at a single point in time for AWP or WAC reported in the year indicated.

Data does not include NDCs for drug products that are co-licensed, co-marketed or repackaged; or for drug ingredients used by pharmacists for compounding prescriptions.

* Data for 2008 was for January 1 through June 30. The number reported above was annualized by doubling the experience from the first 6 months.

Figure 1. Extraordinary Price Increases of Drug Products: 1988 to 2008 Brand Single Source & Brand Off-Patent NDCs.

IMPACT OF *EXTRAORDINARY* DRUG PRICE INCREASES

Obviously there have been some extremely high price increases for a large and growing number of drug products. Because of the magnitude of these *extraordinary* price increases, it is hard to imagine that there has not been a significant impact on the market. These observations raise questions and concerns.

The questions involve asking:

Why have these *extraordinary* price increases occurred?
What market forces have led to, or allowed, these *extraordinary* price increases?

What patterns are there with respect to types of drug products involved?
What patterns are there with respect to types of drug firms involved?
What policy issues are raised by this pricing behavior?
What policy approaches may be appropriate to mitigate or regulate this behavior?

The concerns raised by these *extraordinary* price increases include:

What is the impact Medicare Part D and Part B drug expenditures?
What is the impact on Medicaid drug expenditures?
What is the impact on drug expenditures in other government programs such as the Veterans Administration, the 340 B program, Indian Health Service, the active military health system, and other programs?
What is the impact on employer and private drug benefit programs?
What is the impact on orphan drug products?
What is the impact on access to medications?
What is the impact on access and affordability to vulnerable patient populations?

FACTORS DRIVING *EXTRAORDINARY* DRUG PRICE INCREASES

The pharmaceutical market is extremely complex and vexing to most observers. There are many unique institutional and structural features to the pharmaceutical market that influence the economic behavior of drugs and drug prices. The extent and magnitude of price increases seen in our preliminary study of this issue appear to indicate that the *extraordinary* price increases are not driven by the ordinary explanations for price increases such as the general inflation rate of the economy, the cost of materials, labor and distribution, or the costs of FDA required research for approval.

The magnitude of these *extraordinary* price increases is so great that these prices do not appear to be the product of an economically efficient competitive market. In fact, these prices may well be *supra competitive* prices, that is, prices above what can be sustained in a competitive market. Supra competitive prices are present when a firm has a unique position in a market with respect to intellectual property, legal status, barriers to entry, product features that offer a competitive advantage, or other factors. The number and magnitude of these *extraordinary* price increases also raises the possibility that antitrust issues may be present. Determination of the antitrust implications would require an assessment of the specific and unique market for each drug product to determine the circumstances and market forces that enabled these *extraordinary* price increases to be taken and sustained.

Most of the drug products with *extraordinary* price increases are not among the top 100 to 500 drug products on the market. In part, these drug products may have been able to implement these *extraordinary* price increases because these are low volume drugs that are not often tracked or noticed in the marketplace. In a sense, these drug products and their price increases have "flown below the radar" with respect to attention being given to their pricing behavior.

Many of these drug products are for conditions that have a relatively small volume of demand. Indeed, some of these drug products are even designated as orphan drugs—meaning that they are for conditions that have a small target population. Among the drug products with *extraordinary* price increases are a number of products that are unusual dosage forms such as injections, gels, transdermal patches, sustained release tablets and capsules, and others. Some of these drug products may have such a small market that it would not be profitable for two competitors to survive. Other drug products with *extraordinary* price increases may have been in short supply either before or after the price increase was taken. The fact that some of these drug products are sold only through limited distribution channels (e.g., specialty pharmacies, mail order pharmacies, physician dispensers, dialysis care centers, and others) may also have played a factor in enabling *extraordinary* price increases.

The intellectual property and exclusivity status of these drug products may also have facilitated the *extraordinary* price increases. Among the drugs found to have these large price increases were old drugs that have a patent for a new use of the drug, thus providing a period of market exclusivity for the drug product. Other old drug products have been prepared in a new dosage form that may be the subject of a patent, thus preventing the expected generic competition that is usually seen. In other situations, certain drug firms have a large number of drug products with *extraordinary* price increases. This observation raises the issue of whether or not the extreme price increases are a matter of a particular corporate strategy. Firms may acquire drug products that have limited market competition, or that have high potential for monopoly power with or without intellectual property rights.

The PRIME Institute plans to continue research in this area to better understand and characterize the market conditions that have led to the growth of *extraordinary* price increases for prescription drug products. Our research will look for patterns across drug firms, therapeutic categories, market conditions, intellectual property and exclusivity status, dosage forms, distribution channels and other factors. The continued research will also examine how these *extraordinary* price increases have affected private and government drug programs, market entry and the market for drug products, and specific patient populations.

SUMMARY

Extraordinary price increases for drug products have been observed in recent years. These *extraordinary* price increases are price changes of more than 100% at a single point in time with some ranging to more than a 10,000% increase in price. About one in every twenty brand single source drug products (5.3%) has had one or more *extraordinary* price increases. These enormous price increases certainly affect the individual patients who are using the medication and in aggregate these large price increases expand the ever-growing expenditures of private and public drug programs. The PRIME Institute will continue to study this issue to improve our understanding of the issues involved and to identify policy alternatives to address any societal concerns that may be present.

In: Prescription Drug Pricing
Editors: J. R. Dickson, A. M. Woebler
ISBN: 978-1-61324-639-9

Chapter 7

TESTIMONY OF ALAN L. GOLDBLOOM, MD, PRESIDENT AND CEO, CHILDREN'S HOSPITALS AND CLINICS OF MINNESOTA, BEFORE THE JOINT ECONOMIC COMMITTEE, HEARING ON "AT WHAT COST? EGREGIOUS PRICE INCREASES IN THE PHARMACEUTICAL DRUG INDUSTRY"

Madame Chairman, members of the committee, thank you for the opportunity to testify here today on this critically important issue.

My name is Dr. Alan Goldbloom; I am president and CEO of Children's Hospitals and Clinics of Minnesota. We are the 7th largest pediatric health care system in the nation and we are the largest provider of care to children with severe prematurity, cancer, heart disease, and complex surgical conditions in the Upper Midwest.

Children's of Minnesota is recognized – both nationally and internationally – for our outstanding outcomes in treating premature infants.

My testimony here today will focus on my personal experiences at Children's of Minnesota and two drugs we use in treating premature babies and a rare seizure disorder in very young infants. My testimony is not a rant against the industry as a whole, for this industry has produced extraordinary advances in health care, from which we all benefit. Rather, my concern is focused on the practices of some specialty pharmaceutical companies and the questionable pricing of some older drugs. And though my personal experiences involve two specific companies, they are in no way alone in this practice nor is it confined to only pediatric pharmaceuticals.

One condition we treat in infants is patent ductus arteriosus – or PDA. PDA affects about 3,000 infants annually and is most common in premature babies. I will explain this in very simple terms. Blood circulation changes within minutes of a baby's birth. Normally, our blood picks up oxygen in the lungs and then is pumped by the heart to bring that oxygen to the rest of our body. However, a baby doesn't breath while still in the womb. Instead, a blood vessel called the ductus arteriosus diverts blood away from the lungs, and the fetus actually gets oxygen directly from the mother via the umbilical cord. Once the baby begins to breath after birth, the ductus arteriosus normally spontaneously closes, allowing blood to flow to the newborn's lungs. However, in some babies, especially those who are premature, the ductus does not close. Often, this is a minor problem that resolves without treatment. However, in some infants it becomes serious enough to cause congestive heart failure, and to interfere significantly with breathing. When that happens, treatment is required. Last year, Children's of Minnesota treated around 110 babies for this condition.

For many years, the only way to definitively treat this condition was with surgery, a procedure in which the persistently open artery was simply tied off. However, over 30 years ago it was learned that the drug indomethacin (Indocin), when given intravenously, could often produce the same result without subjecting the baby to surgery. Indocin is now the standard initial treatment for this condition.

Until recently, Indocin has been a low cost, safe, non-surgical way to treat these infants. In fact, the cost for Indocin up until January of 2006 was just over $108 per unit. About 42 of the nation's largest free-standing children's hospitals are members of an organization called Child Health Corporation of America (CHCA), which serves as the group purchasing organization for three-quarters of those hospitals. For the members of the group purchasing organization, the collective annual cost prior to 2006 was just $136,426 nationally.

However, when the specialty pharmaceutical company Ovation bought exclusive rights to Indocin and several other drugs from pharmaceutical giant Merck in August of 2005, the price for one unit of Indocin jumped from $108 to $1,500 – a 1,278 percent increase. Yet Indocin is an old drug. It has been on the market for more than three decades, so this dramatic price increase cannot be attributed to the high cost of research and development. As purchasers, the children's hospitals have had no other options. There have been no other manufacturers of Indocin. Effectively, one company has a monopoly and can use it to price-gouge.

Madame Chairman, at this time I would like to insert into the record the article titled "Drug Pricing in Pediatrics: The Egregious Example of Indomethacin" authored by Dr. Alan Jobe of Cincinnati Children's Hospital in Cincinnati, Ohio which appeared in the Journal of The American Academy of Pediatrics in June of 2007.

On the price increase of Indocin after Ovation acquired the drug from Merck, Dr. Jobe writes "This is a rather astounding increase in price for a drug that has a stable niche market and requires no advertising, no educational expenses (all neonatologists know how to use indomethacin), and no further drug development. It is quite hard to imagine how such an increase in price could be justified." (Pediatrics, Volume 119, Number 6, June 2007, pg. 1197). Dr. Jobe also points out that the cost per milligram of Indocin is 30 to 60 times higher in the United States than other countries that have similar health care systems with little explanation as to why this occurs except for profit motivation. The cost per milligram in the U.S. is $1,875 compared with $14 in Canada, $16 in Britain, $22 in Germany and Holland, and $11 in Australia.

The effect of this dramatic price increase in our hospital has totaled nearly 150,000 dollars in the first year of the price increase. And, according to CHCA it cost its member hospitals close to $2 million that same year – that's up from just over $136,000 just one year earlier. Like all health care providers, we struggle with the issue of increasing costs. Often we are not able to immediately recover these costs from insurers, especially when children's hospitals rely heavily on Medicaid as the single largest insurer of children in the country. Eventually, however, increased costs do get passed on, and are reflected in the premiums that individuals and businesses pay, and in the tax-supported programs like Medicaid. From our perspective, that extra $150,000 that we paid to one drug manufacturer is money we would much rather have spent on improved services for patients.

The children's hospitals who are part of the CHCA group purchasing organization represent only the tip of the iceberg when it comes to the numbers of patients and costs of Indocin in the nearly 600 neonatal intensive care units nationwide. Most of these units are not in children's hospitals, but instead are often in general and maternity hospitals where the babies are born. So the overall impact is ultimately much higher than I have quoted here.

Indocin is not the only drug Ovation has marked up in such a dramatic fashion. Three other drugs that were purchased from Merck – Cosmegen, Diuril Sodium, and Mustargen have seen price increases of 3,437 percent, 864 percent, and 979 percent respectively. Cosmegen is an agent used to treat a variety of pediatric cancers, Diuril Sodium is a diuretic used to reduce fluid overload in infants and neonates, and mustargen is used to treat brain tumors and certain lymphomas (another form of cancer).

Madame Chairman, I would like to insert into the record the following chart that shows the cost of the four drugs purchased by Ovation. As you will see, after Ovation purchased these four drugs from Merck, there was a significant price increase – by as much as 3,437 percent in the case of Cosmegen.

Brand Name	Price per unit Prior to 01/24/06	Price per unit As of 06/08/06	Percent of Increase
Cosmegen	$13.43	$475.05	3437%
Diuril Sodium	$12.36	$119.21	864%
Indocin I.V.	$108.88	$1500.00	1278%
Mustargen	$50.55	$545.28	979%

*Information provided by the Child Health Corporation of America

I would also like to insert the following chart that shows how CHCA member hospitals have been affected by the price increases in these four drugs by Ovation:

Brand Name	2005 Total purchased units	Price per unit prior to 01/24/06	2005 Total Spend	Price per unit as of 06/08/06	2006 Extended Volume
Cosmegen	5,282	$13.43	$70,937.26	$475.05	$2,509,214.10
Diuril Sodium	12,991	$12.36	$160,568.76	$119.21	$1,548,657.11
Indocin I.V.	1,253	$108.88	$136,426.64	$1,500	$1,879,500.00
Mustargen	42	$50.55	$2,123.10	$545.28	$22,901.76
Grand Total	27,195		$370,055.76		$5,960,272.97

*Information provided by the Child Health Corporation of America

Madame Chairman, the total cost increase for CHCA hospitals in one year for these four drugs alone was more than $5.5 million.

One of the best known examples of similar practice in the industry occurred when the specialty pharmaceutical company Questcor bought Acthar

Gel from Aventis. Acthar Gel is used to treat infantile spasms, a rare, severe, and treatment-resistant form of seizures affecting very young infants. Acthar Gel is considered the gold standard in the treatment of IS. At Children's of Minnesota, we have one of the nation's largest, most advanced epilepsy treatment units and have used Acthar Gel nearly 50 times so far this year.

Originally approved in 1978 for multiple sclerosis, the cost of the drug has always been high. However, after Questcor bought the rights to sell Acthar Gel, the price went from a list price of $1,650 per vial to a list price of $23,269 per vial. That's twenty three thousand, not twenty three hundred dollars. In fact, this more than 1,000 percent price increase costs CHCA hospitals more than $21 million per year.

Madame Chairman and Members of the Committee, there are many other drugs – hundreds in fact – that are priced this way – both pediatric and non-pediatric. And, even with good insurance, a twenty percent copay on Acthar Gel is more than many people's mortgage payment. What is frightening is that in this time of skyrocketing health care costs, the burden of expensive health care now affects the insured as well as the uninsured or under insured. The market for many of these drugs is quite limited, so it is unlikely that other companies will begin to produce or sell a low-volume specialty product at a reasonable cost. The resulting monopoly is resulting in windfall profit opportunities for companies like Ovation and Questcor, and they are taking full advantage.

At this time Madame Chairman I would like to place into the record an article dated April 14, 2008 by Gina Kolata that appeared in the New York Times titled "Co-Payments for Expensive Drugs Soar."

Today, the nation is in an uproar over $4 dollar a gallon gasoline. We accuse the nation's oil companies of price gouging and Members of Congress and the presidential candidates are working to find solutions to the problem. But, if you compare the most recent financials for Exxon Mobil and Questcor - you'll find that one company's profit margin is much higher – and it's not who you might think. Pharmaceuticals and specialty pharmaceuticals are the nation's most profitable industries. I want to reiterate that my testimony today is not a rant against the industry as a whole which has produced many extraordinary benefits in health care. Instead, my concern is focused on the practices I just described, in which unjustified pricing decisions are taking advantage of some of the most vulnerable members of our population, and driving health costs up unnecessarily.

Thank you for the opportunity to speak with you today.

In: Prescription Drug Pricing
Editors: J. R. Dickson, A. M. Woebler
ISBN: 978-1-61324-639-9

Chapter 8

TESTIMONY OF DANIELLE FOLTZ, BEFORE THE JOINT ECONOMIC COMMITTEE, HEARING ON "AT WHAT COST? EGREGIOUS PRICE INCREASES IN THE PHARMACEUTICAL DRUG INDUSTRY"

Chairman Schumer, Vice Chair Maloney, Senator Klobuchar and members of the distinguished panel. I am Danielle Foltz of Rhode Island and the mother of Trevor Foltz. I want to thank you for this opportunity to speak today about our family's experience with Infantile Spasms and our journey to receive critically needed treatment for our son.

While I am speaking only on behalf of my own family, I would also like to acknowledge the support of the Epilepsy Foundation. The Epilepsy Foundation represents the 3 million Americans who have epilepsy and their goal is to help those individuals get access to the care they need. I know they will continue to follow this hearing and the path from here forward. Thank you.

I understand that today's hearing is highly political. But for us - and the two thousand families devastated by the diagnosis of Infantile Spasms each year - it's personal.

How do you find the words to describe the most horrific event of your life; your personal valley of the shadow of death? Because that is exactly the feeling that clamps your heart when you are at a place where the medication needed to rescue your child is unattainable.

For 7½ months we celebrated our beautiful third born, Trevor. In fact, we were packing luggage in anticipation of returning to our non-profit ministry & home in Tanzania, East Africa when we noticed the jerky, odd movements Trevor suddenly started making. It resembled a newborn startle reflex.

Devastated does not touch how we felt when we learned that those jerky movements were actually seizures! Trevor was having as many as 20 seizures in a 60 second span; up to 5 times a day. We knew it was serious when the neurologist told us to meet with him immediately following Trevor's first EEG.

In that meeting we were given the devastating news. Our beautiful 7½ month old son had the rare & catastrophic disorder called Infantile Spasms.

All three neurologists we consulted told us the same thing. If we did not get his seizures under control immediately Trevor's developing brain would be irreparably damaged. We were told the only thing between our son and a shot at a normal life was a drug called ACTH, marketed as Acthar gel by Questcor Pharmaceuticals.

Our neurologist prepared us that Trevor's treatment would be pricey. He estimated around $10,000 per vial. We went numb.

We immediately notified our insurance company. The urgency of providing Trevor's treatment was heavy and we needed to move forward as quickly as possible. As Trevor's seizures intensified we read the information about IS online and the sorrow of what we were up against was emotionally overwhelming.

What we didn't know was that 4 months prior to Trevor's diagnosis, Questcor Pharmaceuticals had implemented a new business model. This business model included raising the price per vial of Acthar Gel from approximately $1000 each to over $30,000 a vial. And because Trevor was the first child to require ACTH treatment after the price increase, not even our neurologist was aware of just how dramatically the price had risen. What he thought would cost no more than $50,000 total would now be an astounding $150,000 for the medication alone!

In hindsight, we have no doubt the excessive price of this drug influenced the insurance company against originally approving it for Trevor.

My husband spent days on the phone fighting for Trevor to have coverage. We knew there was no way we could afford to pay for his treatment ourselves. One vial of Acthar was being quoted at a minimum of $30,000. And Trevor needed 5 vials. We could buy a nice 3 bedroom colonial is some areas of the country with that kind of money! But because we had given our lives to serve a non-profit ministry in Tanzania, we don't own that 3 bedroom colonial. We didn't have a house to mortgage as collateral for his treatment – which I've heard some families have been forced to do. All of our earthly possessions were in Africa. We had nothing to liquidate to come up with the money. But to wait was not okay. We needed to save our son NOW.

And so I was frantically looking for other options. Any options.

I called the Acthar support & assistance line because I read that Questcor offers the assurance that no child who truly needs this treatment will go without. I spoke with a call center representative and was informed that the approval process included paper-work for ourselves & Trevor's doctors to submit. When I asked how long the approval process would take I was informed it would be a minimum of 3 business days. When I asked if approval was a sure thing in a case like ours – I was told "no". At that point, my emotions got the best of me, and I informed her that I thought it was a sham! That if Questcor was really about providing a vital medication in a time of desperate need it wouldn't take three business days just to get a maybe!

When your infant's body is being wracked by forty plus seizures daily – you do not have THREE business days to play Russian Roulette waiting for a medication that could stop his seizures and right the world again!

Those days following Trevor's diagnosis were the most emotionally dark in our family's life. My husband & I were pretty much a puddle on the floor. Just getting that kind of a diagnosis shatters you, but then to add the guilt of knowing that you may not be able to rescue your son because you can't afford to? It's un-imaginable and unacceptable.

We literally thought it was possible that our son would go without treatment. Or that he would be forced to use a less effective medication that could leave him developmentally challenged forever. I wonder how many families are living that same nightmare right now? How many are being exploited in their hour of desperation?

Finally, on Wednesday November 21st 2007, the day before Thanksgiving, after numerous emotional phone calls between my husband & our employer we were told to move forward with the treatment. It had already been one day shy of a week since Trevor's diagnosis. And each day without treatment was stealing our son. We witnessed his physical regression and distress as the seizures became more violent.

We were admitted the following day. Trevor's first Thanksgiving was spent at Hasbro Children's Hospital.

Because ACTH must be injected into the thigh, a nurse had to teach us how to administer it once we went home. When she asked my husband if he was nervous about giving Trevor his shot for the first time, he answered that he was more nervous about holding $5000 in a single syringe. Or worse, dropping the vial!

I know that we were lucky. Our insurance ended up covering Trevor's 6 week course of ACTH; which has proven to be his miracle drug. Trevor has been seizure free since his fourth injection. Trevor is the poster child for why this drug needs to be available & affordable! Today we are celebrating our amazing miracle boy! We pray that Trevor will continue to be seizure free. But what if his spasms return? Will we again have to fight for ACTH?

I will leave this hearing today and go home. I'll return to my life of loving & advocating for my son. But my story is in-ex-tricably connected to the 2000 families this year- and the next- and the next - who will live this horrific diagnosis. What about them? My heart cannot help but be consumed for the other families that will be devastated by Infantile Spasms this year. Will they have access to this drug? Or will ACTH not even be an option for their child because they are priced out of the drug they desperately need?

In fact, in preparation for this testimony today my husband researched the current price of a vial of ACTH. Unbelievably, the escalation has not plateaued! The very same vial we ended up paying $26,000 to obtain six months ago, today can cost as much as $40,000. Where does it end? I'm not going to pretend that I understand the many layers of this issue. But what I can wrap my heart around is the terror a mom faces when she cannot rescue her baby. Not because his sickness is un-treatable but because financially she cannot access the medication he needs!

I implore you today to please consider my thoughts and to find a way to help families like mine get access to the medications they need. Please help families dealing with Infantile Spasms get affordable access to the drug that can give them a miracle too.

In: Prescription Drug Pricing
Editors: J. R. Dickson, A. M. Woebler
ISBN: 978-1-61324-639-9

Chapter 9

ENTRY THREATS AND PRICING IN THE GENERIC DRUG INDUSTRY

Brett Wendling*[*] *and Steven Tenn

ABSTRACT

We provide the first analysis of potential competition in the generic drug industry. Our identification strategy exploits a provision of the Hatch-Waxman Act that rewards 180 days of marketing exclusivity to the first generic drug applicant against the holder of a branded drug patent. This provision creates observable drug-level variation in both actual and potential competition that allows us to identify their separate effects. We find mixed evidence of price being used as a strategic entry deterrent. In smaller drug markets where entry is more easily deterred, we find that price falls in response to an increase in potential competition. We also find that few manufacturers enter these markets after the Hatch-Waxman exclusivity period, indicating this price reduction is an effective deterrent. In contrast, in larger drug markets the incumbent accommodates entry by lowering price only after competing manufacturers enter the market.

[*] Corresponding author. *E-mail: bwendling@ftc.gov*. Mailing address: 600 Pennsylvania Ave NW, Washington, DC 20580. We thank Greg Kuczura and Luke Olson for outstanding research assistance, and Abe Dunn, Douglas Herman, Daniel Hosken, David Schmidt, Loren Smith, and Christopher Wheeler for providing helpful comments. The views expressed in this paper are those of the authors and do not necessarily represent the views of the Federal Trade Commission or any individual Commissioner.

Keywords: potential competition, entry deterrence, pharmaceutical, pricing
JEL Classification Codes: L11, L13, L65

ENTRY THREATS AND PRICING IN THE GENERIC DRUG INDUSTRY

I. Introduction

It is well recognized that an incumbent may deter potential competitors by taking strategic action that reduces the profitability of entry. However, the use of price as a strategic entry deterrent is controversial since it may be profitable for the incumbent to raise price after entry has occurred, making its commitment to a low, entry-deterring price incredible. Depending on the theoretical model used to explain the link between the incumbent's pre-entry price and an entrant's expected profits, the effect of potential competition can vary from being extremely strong to entirely ineffectual in constraining market power (Gilbert 1 989a,b). This wide range of theoretical outcomes highlights the need for empirical analysis to determine the real-world importance of potential competition.

Ideally, one would measure the effect of exogenous changes in potential competition after controlling for other relevant industry factors. In practice, however, it has proved difficult to account for changes in potential competition since they are often unobservable. Consequently, empirical evidence of potential competition is far more limited than support for the impact of actual competition (see Section II).

We provide the first analysis of potential competition in the generic drug industry. Our identification strategy exploits the "Drug Price Competition and Patent Term Restoration Act of 1984," commonly known as the Hatch-Waxman Act. This regulation has several provisions that encourage generic entry into prescription drug markets. The provision relevant to our analysis gives generic drug firms incentive to challenge branded drug patents.[1] It allows a generic drug manufacturer to include a "paragraph IV certification" in its Abbreviated New Drug Application (ANDA) to the Food and Drug Administration (FDA) that its version of the drug will either not infringe on the FDA's Orange Book patents, or that the relevant Orange Book patents are invalid.[2] The Hatch-Waxman Act encourages generic firms to incur litigation costs by rewarding 180 days of marketing exclusivity to the first to file an

ANDA with a paragraph IV certification.[3] This marketing exclusivity period protects the designated first-filer from competition with other generic entrants.[4] Following the end of the exclusivity period, two changes occur. First, there may be variation in actual competition as other generic drug manufacturers enter the market. Second, regardless of whether entry occurs, there is the threat of (additional) entry that does not exist during the exclusivity period. Since the Hatch-Waxman Act creates observable variation in both actual and potential competition, we can separately identify their impact on price.

Our analysis of the effect of potential competition on price employs a treatment-control group framework.[5] The treatment group consists of generic drugs that received marketing exclusivity during the initial 180 days. We measure the change in price between the exclusivity period and the following period where the Hatch-Waxman Act does not prohibit entry. When measuring this price change we control for other factors that vary between the two periods, including the number of actual competitors. We compare this to a counterpart price change for drugs that were not granted an exclusivity period. The key difference between the two sets of drugs is that the former experiences a change in potential competition after the first 180 days, while the latter does not. Our "difference in difference" estimator uses this variation to capture the impact of potential competition on generic drug prices.

We find mixed evidence of price being used as a strategic entry deterrent in the generic drug industry. For small drug markets, where it is easier to deter entry due to lower expected profits, we find that price falls in response to an increase in potential competition. Few manufacturers enter these markets following expiration of the Hatch-Waxman exclusivity period, indicating this price reduction is an effective deterrent. In contrast, in larger drug markets where entry deterrence is less likely to be successful, the incumbent maintains a high price until forced to respond to actual competition.

The layout of the paper is as follows. Section II reviews the preceding literature. Section III details the dataset employed. Our identification approach is discussed in Section IV. Section V presents the econometric methodology and reports results. Section VI concludes.

II. Literature Review

In early models of potential competition, the incumbent commits to sell the "limit quantity" (and charges the corresponding "limit price") where the residual demand faced by a potential entrant is insufficient to support profitable entry (Bain 1949, Modigliani 1958, SylosLabini 1962, Dixit 1 979).[6] Factors that affect the feasibility of a limit-pricing strategy include fixed entry costs, returns to scale, and product differentiation. The key assumption in the limit- pricing framework is that the incumbent commits to sell the limit quantity regardless of whether entry actually occurs. This assumption has been criticized in the subsequent literature since, if entry occurs, the profit maximizing strategy for the incumbent may be to accommodate the entrant by reducing output. When this is recognized by a forward-looking potential entrant, limit pricing may not be a credible entry deterrent.[7]

One way of overcoming this weakness of the limit-pricing framework is to incorporate cost uncertainty into the model (Salop 1979, Milgrom and Roberts 1982). If an entrant cannot observe the incumbent's costs, the incumbent may deter entry by setting a low price to signal it is a low cost firm or to hide the fact it is a high cost firm.

An alternative approach to modeling the effect of potential competition is the "contestable markets" theory (Baumol et al. 1982). This framework relies on several strong assumptions that include zero sunk costs of entry and that an entrant can capture the entire market by undercutting the incumbent's price. In a contestable market, a monopolist incumbent is so constrained by potential competition that it cannot make positive profits. Otherwise, entry could profitably occur since the entrant is assumed to have the same costs as the incumbent.

The models described above provide avenues through which potential competition may affect incumbent pricing. However, each model provides a very different description of the nature of potential competition. Moreover, the models characterize conditions under which potential competition does not lead to lower prices. This wide range of theoretical outcomes highlights the need for empirical analysis to determine the importance of potential competition.

Relatively little empirical research examines the effects of potential competition. In their reviews of the literature, Gilbert (1 989a,b) and Bergman (2003) discuss the problem of measuring potential competition and separately identifying its impact from correlated market factors that also affect price. Due to these difficulties, empirical research has largely focused on the airline industry, where institutional factors facilitate the measurement of potential competitors (Morrison and Winston 1987, Strassmann 1990, Kwoka 2001, Goolsbee and Syverson 2008). This research generally finds that the incumbent responds to potential entry by lowering price, but the impact of a potential entrant is less than the effect of a realized entrant. Of course, this finding may not apply to industries that face different competitive conditions.[8]

Empirical Pharmaceutical Literature

The prescription drug industry has been used extensively to evaluate the effect of entry on price. This is due to both the importance of the industry to the overall economy, and because the large number of independent, yet comparable, drug markets facilitates statistical analysis. Researchers generally find the impact of realized entry differs for branded and generic drugs (Caves et al. 1991, Graboski and Vernon 1992, Griliches and Cockburn 1994, Lu and Comanor 1998, Reiffen and Ward 2005, Regan 2008). While generic drug prices decline in the number of generic manufacturers, branded drug prices either increase or stay the same. A related literature finds that generic entry is more likely to occur in larger drug markets (Frank and Salkever 1997, Scott Morton 1999).

A smaller set of papers analyzes the impact of potential competition in the pharmaceutical industry. Ellison and Ellison (2007) develop a theory in which the incumbent's investment is non-monotonic with respect to market size when firms respond to potential entrants. They find support for non-monotonicity with respect to advertising and research and development in branded drug markets. They interpret this result as evidence of incumbent response to potential entry. Bergman and Rudholm (2003) analyze Swedish data and find that branded drug prices decline following an increase in potential competition due to patent expiration. Cool et al. (1999) exploits the New Drug Application (NDA) approval changes in the 1962 amendment to the "Food, Drugs, and Cosmetics Act," as well as the presence of firms in different therapeutic classes, to identify the effects of potential competition on branded drugs.[9] They find that firm profitability is curbed by the threat of competition.

All of these papers analyze the impact of potential competition on branded drugs. To our knowledge, our study is the first to analyze the impact of potential competition on generic drug prices. As noted above, a large number of studies show that the effect of actual competition by generic manufacturers significantly differs for branded and generic drugs. This suggests that the literature's findings regarding potential competition in the branded drug industry may not apply to generic drugs. Consequently, it is important to analyze the effect of potential competition specifically in that industry.

III. Data

Our analysis employs monthly wholesale data from IMS pharmaceutical services. This dataset reports sales for every oral solid prescription medication distributed in the United States over the period January 2003 to December 2008.[10] Sales are reported separately by drug, which is defined as a unique combination of molecule, dosage form, strength, and therapeutic class. The IMS data is combined with information from the FDA regarding when the Hatch-Waxman exclusivity period occurs for each drug (where applicable).

Data from the quarter prior to first generic entry is used to measure the market size of each drug, which is employed in our analysis. Due to this need for pre-entry data, we restrict the dataset to drugs that first faced generic competition after April 2003. We also exclude over-the- counter medications, vitamins and decongestants. These drugs are distributed in sales channels that IMS does not survey. In addition, they often change active ingredients over time, which makes them difficult to track from year to year. These restrictions lead to a data sample of 312 drugs, of which 123 were granted a 180-day exclusivity period under the Hatch-Waxman Act.

A striking feature of the data is that dollar sales are highly skewed. The smallest drug in our sample represents less than a million dollars in annual sales while the largest drug has over $2.5 billion in sales, where market size is measured as annualized branded drug sales in the quarter prior to first generic entry. Market size is a key determinant of the number of entrants in drug markets (Frank and Salkever 1997, Scott Morton 1999). Consequently, in much of our analysis we split the sample by whether a drug's market size is above or below the median. Table 1 shows that, on average, there are 2.7 generic manufacturers in small drug markets compared to 5.8 manufacturers in large drug markets. We consider whether this difference in the number of generic entrants affects the feasibility of using price as a strategic entry deterrent.

We motivate our empirical analysis by comparing price trends for generic drugs with and without an exclusivity period. Following standard practice in the literature (Caves et al. 1991), we scale each generic price by the corresponding branded drug's pre-entry price to arrive at a price measure that can be compared across drugs. For each generic drug d in time t, we calculate $p_{dt} = p^g{}_{dt}/p^b{}_d$, where $p^b{}_d$ and $p^g{}_{dt}$ are branded and generic drug prices, respectively. Note that $p^b{}_d$ does not have a time subscript since it corresponds to the branded drug's price in the quarter prior to generic entry. When calculating the generic drug price $p^g{}_{dt}$ we aggregate across all generic manufacturers of a given drug, weighting by volume sales (i.e., price is calculated as total dollar sales across all generic manufacturers divided by total quantity).

Figure 1 presents the mean price ratio p_{dt} for drugs with and without a Hatch-Waxman exclusivity period. Drugs with an exclusivity period initially set a much higher price. During the Hatch-Waxman exclusivity period, drugs with exclusivity are approximately 30% more expensive, on average. This price difference persists for the full 6-month exclusivity period. After the Hatch-Waxman exclusivity period ends, the two price series start to converge and they are quite similar by month eight. These price trends are the result of changes in both actual and potential competition. Once the Hatch-Waxman exclusivity period ends, additional generic competitors enter the market and there is the threat of future entry. The goal of this study is to determine to what extent the price decline that follows the end of the exclusivity period is due to actual versus potential competition.

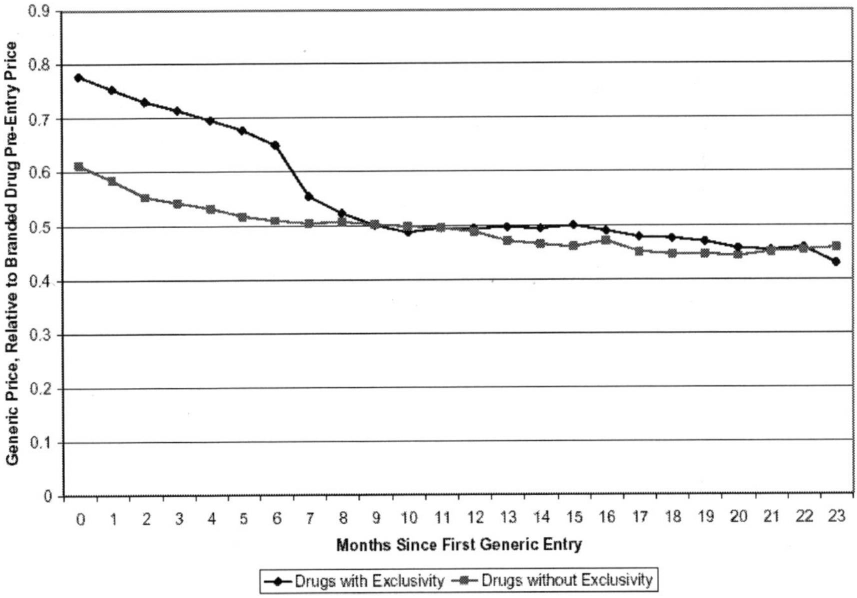

Notes: Branded drug price measured in the quarter prior to first generic entry.

Figure 1. Average Price by Exclusivity.

Table 1. Summary Statistics

	(i) All Drug Markets		(ii) Small Drug Markets		(iii) Large Drug Markets	
	Mean	Std Dev	Mean	Std Dev	Mean	Std Dev
Fixed Characteristics:						
Had an Exclusivity Period	0.39	0.49	0.25	0.43	0.54	0.50
Had an Authorized Generic	0.49	0.50	0.29	0.46	0.68	0.47
Tablet	0.68	0.47	0.68	0.47	0.68	0.47
Capsule	0.12	0.32	0.13	0.34	0.10	0.30
Extended Release Tablet	0.13	0.33	0.10	0.30	0.15	0.36
Extended Release Capsule	0.04	0.18	0.04	0.19	0.03	0.18
Other Dosage Form	0.04	0.21	0.06	0.23	0.03	0.18
Time-varying Characteristics:						
Generic Price, Relative to Branded						
Drug Pre-Entry Price	0.47	0.30	0.57	0.27	0.37	0.28
Months Since First Generic Entry	22.86	16.43	23.02	16.31	22.69	16.54
Number of Generic Manufacturers	4.2	3.4	2.7	2.0	5.8	3.8
Number of Drugs	312		156		156	
Number of Drug-Months	10,787		5,545		5,242	

Notes: IMS wholesale price data, April 2003 to December 2008. Branded drug price is measured in the quarter prior to first generic entry. Market size is measured as annualized branded drug sales in the quarter prior to first generic entry. Drugs with market size above (below) the median are defined as large (small) markets.

IV. The Hatch-Waxman Act and Identification of Potential Competition

In this section, we describe in further detail how the Hatch-Waxman Act allows us to identify the effect of potential competition on generic drug pricing. Consider the following timeline of the first-filing generic manufacturer's incentive to engage in strategic entry deterrence for drugs that enter via a paragraph IV certification.

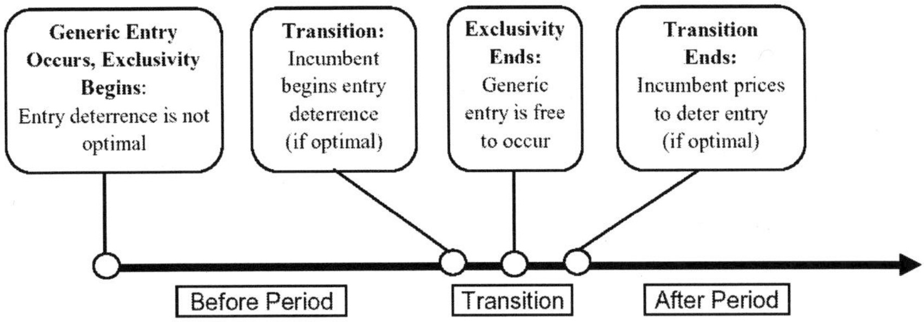

Hatch-Waxman Timeline.

The Hatch-Waxman Act grants a 180-day exclusivity period to the first-filing generic drug applicant against a holder of a branded drug patent. There is little incentive for the first-filer to engage in entry deterrence at the beginning of the exclusivity period. Doing so would be a costly exercise without any offsetting benefit since entry by independent generic firms is prohibited by the Hatch-Waxman Act. After the exclusivity period ends, however, the incumbent firm may find entry deterrence to be a profitable strategy since entry is no longer restricted by the Act.

Although expiration of the exclusivity period clearly delineates when independent firms can enter the market, it is possible that firms initiate entry deterrence prior to the end of exclusivity. This may be the case, for example, if it takes time to implement a price change or if the incumbent wants to signal its pricing strategy to potential entrants. Similarly, the transition to an entry-deterring price may not be finished prior to expiration of the Hatch-Waxman exclusivity period. For these reasons, the pricing strategy during the transition period surrounding expiration of the exclusivity period is likely a mixture of the price strategies employed in the prior and subsequent periods.

An incumbent would like to defer an entry deterring price reduction in order to reap higher profits for as long as possible. Consequently, the transition period surrounding the end of the exclusivity period is likely to be relatively short. However, we are not aware of any institutional market features that provide guidance regarding its duration. Our analysis therefore explores several specifications for the transition period. We employ a 1-month transition window in the baseline model, but also consider a 2-month window as well as no transition period at all.

The analysis compares prices in the "before" period, which consists of the first part of the exclusivity period where entry deterrence is not optimal, to prices in the post-exclusivity "after" period that follows the transition to an entry deterring price (if optimal). Since the pricing strategy during the transition window is unclear, we do not use this period to identify the effect of potential competition. A price decline following expiration of the exclusivity period would be evidence that price is used as a strategic entry deterrent. However, our analysis recognizes that other factors may affect the change in price between these two periods. Most notably, entry may occur. In addition, the Hatch-Waxman exclusivity period is potentially correlated with life-cycle effects that affect drug pricing. To account for these factors we employ a "difference in difference" estimator that compares the change in price for drugs that have an exclusivity period to the price change for drugs that do not.

Specifically, we estimate the effect of potential competition on generic drug prices using a commonly employed two-stage method (Donald and Lang 2007). In the first stage, we calculate each drug's price change after the exclusivity period, or after the first 6 months following initial generic entry for drugs without an exclusivity period. When calculating these price changes we control for other factors that affect price, including changes in actual competition. In the second stage, we test whether the price change for drugs granted an exclusivity period under the Hatch-Waxman Act differs from the price change for non-exclusive drugs. Since the key difference between the two sets of drugs is that one experiences a change in potential competition upon completion of the Hatch-Waxman exclusivity period, while the other does not, our difference in difference estimator measures the effect of potential competition on generic drug prices.

This approach of using a control group, and including additional controls to account for any differences between the two groups, has been widely applied in prior research.[11] Our estimation strategy is closely related to the method used by Bergman and Rudholm (2003) to measure the effect of potential competition on branded drug prices. Bergman and Rudholm use the expiration of the branded drug's patent as a source of variation in potential competition in the same manner we exploit the expiration of the Hatch-Waxman exclusivity period.

A key benefit of the Hatch-Waxman Act is that it provides an exogenous source of variation in potential competition since the Act was written decades prior to the entry events studied in this paper. A second advantage of our study is that we analyze the effect of the Hatch- Waxman Act across a large number of drug markets. Our focus on numerous, independent events that occur at different points in time provides a robust source of variation in potential competition. In addition, the diverse timing of these events allows us to control for calendar time and product life-cycle effects in a flexible manner.

V. Empirical Analysis

Our difference in difference estimator is implemented in two stages. In the first stage, we estimate equation (1) to obtain each drug's change in price between the exclusivity and non-exclusivity periods after controlling for a set of variables X_{dt} that includes the number of competitors in the market as well as other factors (as discussed below).

$$\ln p_{dt}^{g} = \phi_d + \phi_t + \delta_d^0 PRE_{dt} + \delta_d^1 TRANS_{dt} + \delta_d^2 POST_{dt} + X_{dt}\beta + \varepsilon_{dt} \quad (1)$$

Dependent variable $\ln p^g{}_{dt}$ is the log price of generic drug d in month t. Variables ϕ_d and ϕ_t are drug and time fixed effects, respectively. PRE_{dt}, $TRANS_{dt}$, and POS_{dt} are dummy variables for three mutually exclusive periods corresponding to the "before," "transition," and "after" event windows. Note that coefficients $\{\delta^0{}_d, \delta^1{}_d, \delta^2{}_d\}$ for these variables have a drug d subscript indicating a separate effect is estimated for each drug (i.e., we interact PRE_{dt}, $TRANS_{dt}$, and $POST_{dt}$ with a set of drug fixed effects).

We treat a month as being part of the exclusivity period if the end of marketing exclusivity occurs on the 28th day of the month or later. That is, a month is treated as occurring during the exclusivity period only if it is almost entirely composed of exclusive days, with at most three non-exclusive days. The "before" window is defined to correspond to the Hatch- Waxman exclusivity period, or the first 6 months after initial generic entry for drugs without an exclusivity period. The "transition" period is the single month following the before period, which generally contains a mixture of exclusive and non-exclusive days (for drugs with an exclusivity period).[12] The "after" window is the following 12 months.[13]

Equation (1) contains additional variables X_{dt} that control for changes occurring between the before and after periods. This set includes fixed effects for the number of months elapsed since first generic entry. In addition, we control for changes in actual competition by including a set of dummy variables for the number of generic manufacturers.[14] For small drugs, sales sometimes occur irregularly; one or two months without sales can represent standard business practice rather than exit. We assume a manufacturer has exited a particular drug market only after four consecutive months of zero sales.[15] Authorized generics are included in the count of manufacturers.[16] To account for the possibility that the competitive effect of an authorized generic differs from the impact of an independent generic manufacturer (Reiffen and Ward 2007, Federal Trade Commission 2009), we include an indicator for the presence of an authorized generic and interact this variable with the number of generic manufacturers and its square.

Estimates from equation (1) are used to calculate $\Delta \text{ In } p_d = \delta^2_d - \delta^0_d$, the change in log price between the before and after windows after controlling for the number of generic manufacturers and the other variables contained in X_{dt}. This measure is the dependent variable in the second stage of the analysis.[17]

$$\Delta \ln p_d = \alpha EXCL_d + Z_d \gamma + \mu_d \tag{2}$$

Variable $EXCL_d$ is an indicator for whether drug d had an exclusivity period. The model also controls for additional drug characteristics Z_d that potentially explain the change in price between the event windows. This set of additional controls includes an indicator for whether the drug has an authorized generic, the drug's market size percentile, a set of dummy variables for dosage form (tablet, capsule, etc.), and a set of fixed effects for therapeutic class.[18]

The key variable of interest in equation (2) is coefficient a on the exclusivity variable $EXCL_d$. This effect is our "difference in difference" estimator, and measures the change in price between the before and after periods for drugs with exclusivity relative to a control group of non-exclusive drugs. The key identification assumption is that non-exclusive drugs are a valid control group for drugs with an exclusivity period after controlling for variables X_{dt} and Z_d in equations (1) and (2). Any remaining difference between the two sets of drugs is assumed to be due to potential competition; drugs with an exclusivity period face an increase in potential competition after the period ends, which does not occur for their non-exclusive counterparts. Our difference in difference estimator captures this change, allowing us to measure the effect of an increase in potential competition on generic drug prices. We use all non-exclusive drugs as the control group in the baseline model. As a robustness check, later in this section we consider an alternative control group consisting of drugs that submitted a paragraph IV certification but did not receive an exclusivity period.

Table 2. Effect of the Hatch-Waxman Exclusivity Period on Generic Drug Prices

Stage 1 Regression Dep Variable: Log Price		
	Est	SE
Authorized Generic (AG) Present	0.514	0.176*
AG × # Manufacturers	-0.109	0.055*
AG × # Manufacturers Squared	0.005	0.003
Manufacturers = 2	-0.091	0.035*
Manufacturers = 3	-0.087	0.056
Manufacturers = 4	-0.109	0.065
Manufacturers = 5	-0.221	0.077*
Manufacturers = 6	-0.295	0.082*
Manufacturers = 7	-0.362	0.108*
Manufacturers = 8	-0.406	0.126*
Manufacturers = 9	-0.455	0.152*
Manufacturers = 10	-0.581	0.173*
Manufacturers > 10	-0.819	0.246*
Stage 2 Regression Dep Variable: Change in Log Price After Exclusivity Ends		
	Est	**SE**
Had an Exclusivity Period	-0.118	0.084
Had an Authorized Generic	0.039	0.087
Market Size Percentile	-0.581	0.131*
Capsule	-0.106	0.146
Extended Release Tablet	0.168	0.060*
Extended Release Capsule	0.006	0.089
Other Dosage Form	-0.237	0.152

Notes: Robust standard errors are reported that cluster by molecule. Statistical significance: *=5%.

Stage 1 Notes: The model also includes a set of drug fixed effects, time fixed effects, and a set of fixed effects for the number of months elapsed since first generic entry. In addition, for each drug it includes dummy variables for the before, transition, and after event windows. N=10,787 drug-months, R^2=.98, RMSE=.21.

Stage 2 Notes: The model also includes a set of fixed effects for therapeutic class. The dependent variable is estimated from the first stage regression. N=281 drugs, R^2=.47, RMSE=.33.

Table 2 presents the first and second stage regression estimates. Robust standard errors are reported that cluster by molecule. This accounts for any correlation in unobserved characteristics across drugs with the same active ingredient. The first stage results demonstrate the importance of controlling for realized competition. Consistent with prior research, we find that additional competitors lead to lower prices. However, some of the individual coefficients are imprecisely estimated and are not always statistically significant at conventional levels. Competitor type also matters. Generic drug prices are higher when one of the competing manufacturers is an authorized generic, although this effect decreases in the number of competitors.[19]

In the second stage results, the key effect of interest is the coefficient for whether a drug had an exclusivity period, which is our difference in difference estimator. The price of exclusive drugs falls by 11.8% (SE=8.4%) after the exclusivity period ends, relative to the price change for non-exclusive drugs. However, this effect is not statistically significant at any conventional level.

A key determinant of whether a firm engages in strategic entry deterrence is the cost of deterring potential competitors. It is likely that entry deterrence is costlier in large markets, due to their greater profitability. Consequently, an entry-deterring pricing strategy may not be profit maximizing in these markets. To test this hypothesis we split the sample by market size. Drugs with market size above and below the median are referred to as "large" and "small" markets, respectively.

Table 3 reports results from estimating the model separately for small and large drug markets. The effect of the exclusivity period is very different for the two sets of drugs. In small drug markets, the price of exclusive drugs falls by 19.4% (SE=9.2%) relative to non-exclusive drugs. This effect is statistically significant at the 5% level. In contrast, in larger drug markets price does not change in response to potential competition. This finding is consistent with the hypothesis that it is not profitable to deter entry in larger markets where entry is highly likely to occur. Instead, the incumbent generic manufacturer reduces price only when forced to respond to actual entry.

These results suggest that price is used as an entry deterrent in small drug markets, but not in large drug markets. We now explore whether price is an *effective* entry deterrent by estimating equations (1) and (2) using the log number of manufacturers as the dependent variable, rather than price.[20] If price is an effective entry deterrent in small drug markets, one should see relatively little entry following the end of the exclusivity period. Similarly, if firms accommodate entry in large drug markets then entry should be observed following the end of exclusivity in those markets.

Table 3. Effect of the Hatch-Waxman Exclusivity Period on Generic Drug Prices, Separately by Small and Large Drug Markets

Stage 1 Regression Dep Variable: Log Price				
	Small Drug Markets		**Large Drug Markets**	
	Est	**SE**	**Est**	**SE**
Authorized Generic (AG) Present	0.185	0.099	0.733	0.258*
AG × # Manufacturers	-0.023	0.053	-0.174	0.061*
AG × # Manufacturers Squared	0.006	0.005	0.008	0.003*
Manufacturers = 2	-0.038	0.026	-0.181	0.117
Manufacturers = 3	-0.046	0.050	-0.183	0.107
Manufacturers = 4	-0.099	0.079	-0.198	0.098*
Manufacturers = 5	-0.195	0.094*	-0.332	0.095*
Manufacturers = 6	-0.387	0.102*	-0.300	0.102*
Manufacturers = 7	-0.479	0.138*	-0.351	0.128*
Manufacturers = 8	-0.598	0.175*	-0.381	0.144*
Manufacturers = 9	-0.614	0.189*	-0.424	0.154*
Manufacturers = 10	-0.612	0.182*	-0.536	0.176*
Manufacturers > 10	-0.754	0.252*	-0.799	0.227*
Stage 2 Regression Dep Variable: Change in Log Price After Exclusivity Ends				
	Small Drug Markets		**Large Drug Markets**	
	Est	**SE**	**Est**	**SE**
Had an Exclusivity Period	-0.194	0.092*	0.000	0.108
Had an Authorized Generic	-0.066	0.070	0.065	0.138
Market Size Percentile	-0.374	0.202	-0.752	0.307*
Capsule	-0.123	0.128	-0.126	0.215
Extended Release Tablet	-0.012	0.054	0.278	0.095*
Extended Release Capsule	0.011	0.065	-0.014	0.094
Other Dosage Form	-0.114	0.111	-0.165	0.363

Notes: Robust standard errors are reported that cluster by molecule. Statistical significance: *=5%.

Stage 1 Notes: The model also includes a set of drug fixed effects, time fixed effects, and a set of fixed effects for the number of months elapsed since first generic entry. In addition, for each drug it includes dummy variables for the before, transition, and after event windows. Small drug markets: N=5,545 drug-months, R^2=.99, RMSE=. 12. Large drug markets: N=5,242 drug-months, R^2=.98, RMSE=.27.

Stage 2 Notes: The model also includes a set of fixed effects for therapeutic class. The dependent variable is estimated from the first stage regression. Small drug markets: N=141 drugs, R^2=.30, RMSE=.26. Large drug markets: N=140 drugs, R^2=.41, RMSE=.40.

The results from this analysis, reported in Table 4, are consistent with price being used as an entry deterrent in small but not large drug markets. Substantial entry is observed in large drug markets, with a 43.2% (SE=16.2%) increase in the number of manufacturers, relative to the change for non-exclusive drugs. In contrast, only a 15.4% (SE=13.4%) change is found in small drug markets, which is not statistically significant at any conventional level. For smaller drugs we cannot reject the hypothesis that the price reduction following an increase in potential competition is an effective entry deterrent.

Sensitivity Analysis

Recall that in our baseline specification we use a 1-month transition period and a 12- month after period. We now examine the robustness of our results to alternative definitions for these event windows. Specifically, we consider using 0, 1, and 2 transition months, and after windows of 6, 12, and 24 months.

The results of these robustness checks are reported in the first column of Table 5. As before, we find that for small drugs price falls in response to potential competition. The estimated price decline ranges from 15% to 22%, depending on the specification. The only instance where the effect of potential competition is not statistically significant at the 5% level is when a 2-month transition window is used in conjunction with a 6-month after window. Nonetheless, this effect is nearly statistically significant with a p-value of .051. As before, little price change is apparent in large drug markets. The point estimates are generally small in magnitude and are never statistically significant at any conventional level.

In the baseline model, we employ a control group consisting of all non-exclusive drugs. A potential problem is that manufacturers do not randomly decide which drugs should undergo a paragraph IV certification. Patent litigation is costly, and is more likely to be profitable when the expected return from a successful patent challenge is higher. As such, exclusive drugs tend to have a larger market size than non-exclusive drugs. Our analysis accounts for this difference by explicitly controlling for market size. Nonetheless, we recognize the possibility that unobservable differences between the treatment and control groups may remain, potentially biasing our results.

Table 4. Effect of the Hatch-Waxman Exclusivity Period on Number of Generic Manufacturers, Separately by Small and Large Drug Markets

Stage 2 Regression Dep Variable: Change in Log Manufacturers After Exclusivity Ends				
	Small Drug Markets		Large Drug Markets	
	Est	SE	Est	SE
Had an Exclusivity Period	0.154	0.134	0.432	0.162*
Market Size Percentile	0.544	0.242*	0.968	0.381*
Capsule	0.083	0.134	0.181	0.334
Extended Release Tablet	0.265	0.213	-0.251	0.122*
Extended Release Capsule	-0.072	0.158	-0.029	0.186
Other Dosage Form	-0.215	0.190	-0.368	0.145*

Notes: Robust standard errors are reported that cluster by molecule. Statistical significance: *=5%.

Stage 1 Notes: The model includes a set of drug fixed effects, time fixed effects, and a set of fixed effects for the number of months elapsed since first generic entry. In addition, for each drug it includes dummy variables for the before, transition, and after event windows. Small drug markets: N=5,545 drug-months, R^2=.96, RMSE=.21. Large drug markets: N=5,242 drug-months, R^2=.99, RMSE=.22.

Stage 2 Notes: The model also includes a set of fixed effects for therapeutic class. The dependent variable is estimated from the first stage regression. Small drug markets: N=141 drugs, R^2=. 17, RMSE=.39. Large drug markets: N=140 drugs, R^2=.42, RMSE=.50.

We now consider an alternative control group that consists of non-exclusive drugs that filed a paragraph IV certification but did not have a Hatch-Waxman exclusivity period. This occurs when the first-to-file generic firm loses the patent litigation, or reaches a settlement with the branded manufacturer prior to entry.[21] These non-exclusive drugs are more similar to exclusive drugs since both had a paragraph IV certification. Evidence of this is seen in the market size of the two sets of drugs; we could not reject, at any conventional level, the hypothesis that exclusive drugs have the same average market size as non-exclusive paragraph IV drugs.[22] The endogeneity of which drugs are certified under paragraph IV does not pose a problem to the analysis when this alternative control group is employed since both the treatment and control groups undergo the same selection process. The drawback of this alternative control group is that it is substantially smaller, leading to less precise results.[23]

The second column of results in Table 5 repeats the analysis after restricting the dataset to drugs with a paragraph IV certification. For small drug markets, the alternative control group leads to stronger results. The estimated price decline ranges from 22% to 29%, depending on the specification. Each estimate is statistically significant at the 5% level. As before, we do not find a statistically significant effect in large drug markets.

Table 5. Effect of the Hatch-Waxman Exclusivity Period on Generic Drug Prices, Alternative Event Windows and Control Groups

Transition Period	After Period	Control Group 1: All Non-Exclusive Drugs				Control Group 2: Non-Exclusive Paragraph IV Drugs			
		Small Drug Markets		Large Drug Markets		Small Drug Markets		Large Drug Markets	
		Est	SE	Est	SE	Est	SE	Est	SE
None	6 months	-0.147	0.068*	0.002	0.079	-0.215	0.096*	-0.108	0.103
None	12 months	-0.168	0.076*	0.021	0.088	-0.239	0.096*	-0.079	0.108
None	24 months	-0.197	0.082*	0.059	0.098	-0.265	0.103*	-0.010	0.123
1 month	6 months	-0.169	0.082*	-0.033	0.097	-0.265	0.114*	-0.160	0.131
1 month	12 months	-0.194	0.092*	0.000	0.108	-0.275	0.120*	-0.127	0.127
1 month	24 months	0.218	0.096*	0.046	0.118	0.294	0.129*	0.029	0.141
2 months	6 months	-0.176	0.089	-0.040	0.116	-0.272	0.109*	-0.175	0.149
2 months	12 months	-0.203	0.100*	-0.022	0.124	-0.260	0.117*	-0.150	0.152
2 months	24 months	-0.217	0.102*	0.035	0.136	-0.259	0.124*	-0.049	0.175

Notes: Robust standard errors are reported that cluster by molecule. Statistical significance: *=5%. Each estimate corresponds to the coefficient for the "Had an Exclusivity Period" variable from the stage 2 regression. The model with a transition period of 1 month, an after period of 12 months, and using control group 1 corresponds to the baseline specification reported in Table 3.

Table 6 reports the results of similar robustness checks using the log number of manufacturers as the dependent variable. Qualitatively similar, but less precise, estimates are again obtained. The difference with our earlier set of results is that the change in the number of manufacturers in large drug markets is not statistically significant in one specification. However, it is almost significant at the 5% level with a p-value of .051. Generally, the results using the paragraph IV drugs confirm the findings from our baseline specification. In small markets, where entry deterrent pricing is observed, there is little change in the number of competitors. We cannot reject the hypothesis that price is an effective entry deterrent in these markets. In contrast, in large drug markets where entry deterrence is not observed, the number of manufacturers increases after the exclusivity period expires.

As a final robustness check, we undertake the following falsification test. Rather than comparing the price change between the before and after periods, we compute the price change between the after period and a "post-after" window corresponding to the following 12 months. We estimate the same model as before, but now include a post-after indicator variable for each drug. For both exclusive and non-exclusive drugs, there is no change in potential competition between these two periods since the after and post-after windows both follow expiration of the Hatch-Waxman exclusivity period. If the control group is valid then this test should not reveal a significant difference between the treatment and control groups.

Table 6. Effect of the Hatch-Waxman Exclusivity Period on Number of Manufacturers, Alternative Event Windows and Control Groups

Transition Period	After Period	Control Group 1: All Non-Exclusive Drugs				Control Group 2: Non-Exclusive Paragraph IV Drugs			
		Small Drug Markets		Large Drug Markets		Small Drug Markets		Large Drug Markets	
		Est	SE	Est	SE	Est	SE	Est	SE
None	6 months	0.180	0.118	0.386	0.126*	-0.050	0.199	0.404	0.130*
None	12 months	0.150	0.126	0.406	0.147*	-0.050	0.201	0.395	0.160*
None	24 months	0.160	0.119	0.486	0.160*	-0.026	0.197	0.454	0.185*
1 month	6 months	0.196	0.129	0.429	0.136*	-0.080	0.224	0.434	0.145*
1 month	12 months	0.154	0.134	0.432	0.162*	-0.051	0.224	0.411	0.183*
1 month	24 months	0.169	0.124	0.515	0.171*	-0.021	0.219	0.473	0.204*
2 months	6 months	0.171	0.134	0.493	0.171*	-0.141	0.255	0.498	0.200*
2 months	12 months	0.125	0.137	0.501	0.195*	-0.098	0.252	0.481	0.238
2 months	24 months	0.146	0.126	0.595	0.202*	-0.088	0.245	0.562	0.268*

Notes: Robust standard errors are reported that cluster by molecule. Statistical significance: *=5%. Each estimate corresponds to the coefficient for the "Had an Exclusivity Period" variable from the stage 2 regression. The model with a transition period of 1 month, an after period of 12 months, and using control group 1 corresponds to the baseline specification reported in Table 4.

The results from this analysis are generally supportive of our two control groups (nonexclusive drugs and non-exclusive paragraph IV drugs).[24] In the log price regressions, we do not find a statistically significant difference between the treatment and control groups. For smaller drug markets, this is also the case for the log manufacturer regressions. The falsification test "fails" only for large drug markets when all non-exclusive drugs are employed as the control group.[25] The difference in difference estimate for this specification equals 18.1% (SE=7. 8%), indicating that exclusive drugs have significantly more entry between the after and post-after windows than their non-exclusive counterparts. This suggests that it takes more than 12 months for entrants to respond fully to the expiration of the exclusivity period. Apart from this exception, however, the results from the falsification test are consistent with our control groups being valid.

CONCLUSION

The importance of potential competition in constraining market power has long been recognized as a theoretical matter. However, empirical evidence regarding the effects of potential competition is relatively limited despite its importance in understanding the strategic behavior of firms. We add to the empirical literature by providing the first analysis of potential competition in the generic drug industry. This industry offers a large number of independent, yet comparable, drug markets that facilitate statistical analysis. Our identification strategy uses the Hatch-Waxman 180-day exclusivity period granted to the first generic drug applicant against a holder of a branded drug patent as an exogenous source of variation in potential competition that varies over time and across drugs.

Our analysis finds that the incumbent in smaller drug markets lowers price in response to an increase in potential competition, and this price reduction appears to be an effective entry deterrent. In larger drug markets, the incumbent accommodates entry by lowering price only after competing manufacturers enter the market. This pricing strategy leads to a significant increase in the number of competitors once the Hatch-Waxman exclusivity period ends. Overall, the results suggest that price can be an effective entry deterrent in certain circumstances where the cost of deterring entry is not too high.

REFERENCES

Bain, Joe S. (1949). "A Note on Pricing in Monopoly and Oligopoly," *American Economic Review, 39(2)*, 448-64.

Baumol, William J., John C. Panzar & Robert D. Willig. (1982). *Contestable Markets and the Theory of Industry Structure*. New York: Harcourt, Brace, Jovanovich.

Bergman, Mats A. (2003). "*Potential Competition: Theory, Empirical Evidence, and Legal Practice*," Working Paper, Swedish Competition Authority.

Bergman, Mats A. & Niklas Rudholm. (2003). "The Relative Importance of Actual and Potential Competition: Empirical Evidence from the Pharmaceuticals Market," *Journal of Industrial Economics, 51(4)*, 455-67.

Berndt, Ernst R. (2002). "Pharmaceuticals in U.S. Health Care: Determinants of Quantity and Price," *Journal of Economic Perspectives, 16(4)*, 45-66.

Bertrand, Marianne, Esther Duflo & Sendhil Mullainathan. (2004). "How Much Should We Trust Differences-in-Differences Estimates?" *Quarterly Journal of Economics, 119(1)*, 249-75.

Caves, Richard E., Michael D. Whinston & Mark A. Hurwitz. (1991). "Patent Expiration, Entry, and Competition in the U.S. Pharmaceutical Industry," *Brookings Papers on Economic Activity. Microeconomics* 1-66.

Cool, Karel, Lars-Hendrik Roller & Benoit Leleux. (1999). "The Relative Impact of Actual and Potential Rivalry on Firm Profitability in the Pharmaceutical Industry," *Strategic Management Journal, 20(1)*, 1-14.

Dixit, Avinash. (1979). "A Model of Duopoly Suggesting a Theory of Entry Barriers," *Bell Journal of Economics, 10(1)*, 20-32.

Dixit, Avinash. (1980). "The Role of Investment in Entry-Deterrence," *Economic Journal, 90(357)*, 95-106.

Donald, Stephen G. & Kevin Lang. (2007). "Inference with Difference-in-Differences and Other Panel Data," *Review of Economics and Statistics, 89(2)*, 221-33.

Ellison, Glenn & Sara Fisher Ellison. (2007). "Strategic Entry Deterrence and the Behavior of Pharmaceutical Incumbents Prior to Patent Expiration," NBER Working Paper 13069.

Federal Trade Commission. (2009). *Authorized Generics: An Interim Report*. Available at: http://www.ftc.gov/os/2009/06/P062105authorizedgenericsreport.pdf

Federal Trade Commission Staff Report. (2010). *Pay-for-Delay: How Drug Company Pay-Offs Cost Consumers Billions*. Available at: http://www.ftc.gov/os/2010/01/100112payfordelayrpt.pdf

Frank, Richard G. & David S. Salkever. (1997). "Generic Entry and the Pricing of Pharmaceuticals," *Journal of Economics and Management Strategy, 6(1)*, 75-90.

Gaskins, Darius W. (1971). "Dynamic Limit Pricing: Optimal Pricing under Threat of Entry," *Journal of Economic Theory, 3(3)*, 306-22.

Gilbert, Richard J. (1989a). "The Role of Potential Competition in Industrial Organization," *Journal of Economic Perspectives, 3(3)*, 107-27.

Gilbert, Richard J. (1989b). "Mobility Barriers and the Value of Incumbency," in *Handbook of Industrial Organization,* vol. 1, Richard Schmalensee and Robert Willig, eds. New York: North Holland.

Goolsbee, Austan & Chad Syverson. (2008). "How Do Incumbents Respond to the Threat of Entry? Evidence from the Major Airlines," *Quarterly Journal of Economics, 123(4)*, 1611- 33.

Grabowski, Henry G. & John M. Vernon. (1992). "Brand Loyalty, Entry, and Price Competition in Pharmaceuticals after the 1984 Drug Act," *Journal of Law and Economics, 35(2)*, 33 1-50.

Griliches, Zvi & Ian Cockburn. (1994). "Generics and New Goods in Pharmaceutical Price Indexes," *American Economic Review, 84(5)*, 1213-32.

Judd, Kenneth L & Bruce C. Petersen. (1986). "Dynamic Limit Pricing and Internal Finance," *Journal of Economic Theory, 39(2)*, 368-99.

Kwoka, John E. (2001). "Non-Incumbent Competition: Mergers Involving Constraining and Prospective Competitors," *Case Western Law Review, 52*,173-209.

Lee, Jongsu, Yeonbae Kim, Jeong-Dong Lee & Yuri Park. (2006). "Estimating the Extent of Potential Competition in the Korean Mobile Telecommunications Market: Switching Costs and Number Portability," *International Journal of Industrial Organization, 24(1)*, 107-24.

Lu, Z. John & William S. Comanor. (1998). "Strategic Pricing of New Pharmaceuticals," *Review of Economics and Statistics, 80(1)*, 108-18.

Milgrom, Paul and John Roberts. 1982. "Limit Pricing and Entry under Incomplete Information: An Equilibrium Analysis," *Econometrica, 50(2)*, 443-59.

Modigliani, Franco. (1958). "New Developments on the Oligopoly Front," *Journal of Political Economy, 66(3)*, 215-32.

Morrison, Steven A. & Clifford Winston. (1987). "Empirical Implications and Tests of the Contestability Hypothesis," *Journal of Law and Economics, 30(1)*, 53-66.

Regan, Tracy L. (2008). "Generic Entry, Price Competition, and Market Segmentation in the Prescription Drug Market," *International Journal of Industrial Organization, 26(4)*, 930- 48.

Reiffen, David & Michael R. Ward. (2005). "Generic Drug Industry

Dynamics," *Review of Economics and Statistics, 87(1)*, 37-49.

Reiffen, David & Michael R. Ward. (2007). "'Branded Generics' as a Strategy to Limit Cannibalization of Pharmaceutical Markets," *Managerial and Decision Economics, 28(4/5)*, 25 1-65.

Salop, Steven C. (1979). "Strategic Entry Deterrence," *American Economic Review, 69(2)*, 335- 38.

Savage, Scott J. & Michael Wirth. (2005). "Price, Programming and Potential Competition in US Cable Television Markets," *Journal of Regulatory Economics, 27(1)*, 25-46.

Scott Morton, Fiona M. (1999). "Entry Decisions in the Generic Pharmaceutical Industry," *RAND Journal of Economics, 30(3)*, 421-40.

Spence, A. Michael. (1977). "Entry, Capacity, Investment and Oligopolistic Pricing," *Bell Journal of Economics, 8(2)*, 534-44.

Strassmann, Diana L. (1990). "Potential Competition in the Deregulated Airlines," *Review of Economics and Statistics, 72(4)*, 696-702.

Sylos-Labini, Paolo. (1962). *Oligopoly and Technical Progress*. Cambridge: Harvard University Press.

End Notes

[1] The more widely known provision of the Act replaces the original generic drug approval process with an Abbreviated New Drug Application. This regulatory change significantly increased generic entry (Berndt 2002).

[2] In these instances, the FDA may not approve the generic drug until 30 months after the generic files its drug application with the FDA or after a favorable decision in the patent litigation, if earlier.

[3] Prior to 2003, the first-to-file generic manufacturer could be distinguished by the exact minute a drug application was submitted. If several firms provided valid applications on the same day, the FDA would grant exclusivity to the first applicant. This provision has since been relaxed and now multiple firms can be designated as the first-filer.

[4] As noted in footnote 3, the FDA may designate multiple manufacturers as the first-filer. Note, however, that this will not lead to variation in the number of manufacturers within the exclusivity period since additional entry is prohibited by the Hatch-Waxman Act. The only exception is the Act does not stop the branded drug manufacturer from introducing an "authorized generic" during the exclusivity period. Authorized generics typically enter at the beginning of exclusivity, leading to little variation in competition within the period.

[5] Generic drugs are homogenous products with little differentiation across manufacturers. As such, entry deterrence is most likely to occur along the price dimension.

[6] See Gilbert (1989a,b) and Bergman (2003) for discussion of strategic entry deterrence via non-price mechanisms. For example, Spence (1977) and Dixit (1980) analyze investment in capacity.

[7] See also the literature on "dynamic limit pricing" (Gaskins 1971, Judd and Peterson 1986). A limitation of this group of models is that the link between the incumbent's price and the likelihood of future entry is exogenously specified or restricted in a particular way.

[8] A few papers examine the effect of potential competition in other industries. For example, Savage and Wirth (2005) and Lee et al. (2006) consider the cable television and telecommunications industries, respectively. Below, we discuss papers that focus on prescription drugs.

[9] The change required firms to provide evidence that a drug is both safe and efficacious. Prior to the enactment of this law, drug firms only had to demonstrate their product was safe.

[10] An "oral solid" is a drug sold in tablet or capsule form.

[11] See Bertrand et al. (2004) and the citations contained therein for discussion of the "difference in difference" estimation approach. Bertrand et al. recommend the two-stage estimation strategy that we employ.

[12] Later in this section, we consider alternative definitions for the transition period.

[13] The period following the after window is the omitted time category.

[14] When counting the number of manufacturers we exclude drug repackagers.

[15] The date of exit is backdated to the period following the last observed sale. For example, if a manufacturer has positive sales in month 4, but zero sales in months 5-8, then that manufacturer is considered to have exited between month 4 and 5.

[16] An "authorized generic" is a drug approved by the FDA as a branded drug, but marketed as a generic.

[17] In equation 2, each observation corresponds to a particular drug (in contrast, in equation 1 an observation is a drug-month combination). It is not possible to calculate A ln *pd* for 31 drugs where first generic entry occurs in the last 7 months of the data (June 2008 or later), since the after period is never observed. The second stage regression includes 281 drugs from the full sample of 312.

[18] Therapeutic classes with fewer than five drugs in a given regression are grouped together into an "other" category. As before, market size is measured as the corresponding branded drug's annualized sales in the quarter prior to first generic entry.

[19] While the coefficient estimate for the authorized generic dummy may appear to suggest that prices are considerably higher in markets with an authorized generic, the interactions between the authorized generic dummy and the number of manufacturers dampen this effect. In the average market with 4.2 manufacturers, the net impact on price of an authorized generic, holding the total number of manufacturers constant, is 13.8% (SE=8.1%), which is not statistically significant at the 5% level. The net impact of an authorized generic is statistically significant only when there are three or fewer manufacturers (including the authorized generic).

[20] Of course, controls for the number of manufacturers are omitted from the model.

[21] Patent settlements involving paragraph IV drugs are generally agreements on when the first-filing generic firm may enter the market. The settlements do not involve post-entry activity such as pricing. See Federal Trade Commission (2010) for details.

[22] In contrast, when the control group consists of all non-exclusive drugs the difference in means is statistically significant at the 1% level.

[23] Restricting the data to drugs with a paragraph IV certification leads to a sample of 195 drugs.

[24] We conduct the falsification test using the baseline model employed earlier in this section that has a 1- month transition and a 12-month after period. On average, we observe 34 months of data for each drug. It is not practical to use a 24-month after window since relatively few drugs would have much post-after data, since that period starts in month 32 (6 month before window plus a 1 month transition plus a 24 month after window). Use of a 2-month transition window or no transition at all leads to similar results.

[25] The test "passes" when non-exclusive paragraph IV drugs are the controls.

CHAPTER SOURCES

The following chapters have been previously published:

Chapter 1 – This is an edited reformatted and augmented version of a United States Government Accountability Office publication, report GAO-11-306R, dated February 10, 2011.

Chapter 2 - This is an edited reformatted and augmented version of a United States Government Accountability Office publication, report GAO-10-201, dated December 2009.

Chapter 3 - This is an edited reformatted and augmented version of a United States Government Accountability Office publication, report GAO-09-819T, dated June 24, 2009.

Chapter 4 – These remarks were delivered as testimony given on July 24, 2008. U.S. Senator Amy Klobuchar.

Chapter 5 – These remarks were delivered as testimony given on July 24, 2008. Senator Charles E. Schumer, Chairman, Joint Economic Committee.

Chapter 6 – These remarks were delivered as testimony given on July 24, 2008. Madeline M. Carpinelli, research fellow and Stephen W. Schondelmeyer Professor and Director, before Joint Economic Committee, United States Congress.

Chapter 7 – These remarks were delivered as testimony given on July 24, 2008. Alan L. Goldbloom, MD, President and CEO, Children's Hospitals and Clinics of Minnesota before Joint Economic Committee.

Chapter 8 – These remarks were delivered as testimony given on July 24, 2008. Danielle Foltz, mother of Trevor Foltz.

Chapter 9 – This is an edited reformatted and augmented version of a Federal Trade Commission publication, report 301, dated June 2010.

INDEX

A

B

C

D

E

F

G

H

S

T

U

V